Bolles
+
Wilson

Mit Photographien von
With photographs by
Christian Richters

Bolles + Wilson

Neue Bauten und Projekte

Recent Buildings and Projects

Birkhäuser Verlag
Basel · Boston · Berlin

Essays / Essays	6	
	Made in Münster / Made in Münster	
	10	
	Kräne in Berlin und Rotterdam / Cranes in Berlin and Rotterdam	
	12	
	Masse im Medienzeitalter / Mass in the Age of Media	
Projekte / Projects	18	
	Bürogebäude WLV / Office Building WLV (Münster)	
	42	
	Kundenzentrum Zumtobel/Staff / Customer Centre Zumtobel/Staff (Lemgo)	
	50	
	Verwaltungsgebäude WLV / Administration Building WLV (Münster)	
	52	
	Wohnprojekte / Residential Projects (Duisburg; Münster; Castrop-Rauxel)	
	60	
	Eurolandschaft / Euro-Landscape	
	68	
	Medizinisches Dienstleistungszentrum / Medical Service Centre (Castrop-Rauxel)	
	72	
	Dienstleistungszentrum / Business Service Centre (Castrop-Rauxel)	
	82	
	Albeda Schule / Albeda College (Rotterdam)	
	86	
	Hotel New York, Kai-Landschaftsgestaltung / Hotel New York, Quay Landscaping (Rotterdam)	
	88	
	Kop van Zuid, Kai-Landschaftsgestaltung / Kop van Zuid, Quay Landscaping (Rotterdam)	
	106	
	Neues Luxor Theater / New Luxor Theatre (Rotterdam)	
	116	
	Brink Viertel / Brink Centre (Hengelo)	
Anhang / Appendix	122	
	Biographien / Biographies	
	124	
	Mitarbeiter 1994–97 / Collaborators 1994–97	
	126	
	Auswahlbibliographie / Selected Bibliography	
	127	
	Bildnachweis / Illustration Credits	

Made in Münster

Die sechs vor kurzem fertiggestellten Gebäude und andere hier vorgestellte Projekte begründen eine zweite Generation des in Münster ansässigen Büros von Bolles+Wilson. Blickt man auf die Eröffnung der umstrittenen Stadtbücherei Münster im Jahr 1993 zurück, so zeugen die jüngeren Werke von einer Verlagerung der Interessen. Besonders beim Bürogebäude Warendorfer Straße zeigt sich ein neues Insistieren auf Masse, auf das architektonische Objekt. Das Albeda College in Rotterdam ist ein weiteres Beispiel für diese Gebäude. Auch wenn sie vielleicht von der Topographie und den Gezeiten ihres nebulösen Kontextes mitgeformt wurden, so nehmen diese scharf definierten Objekte durch ihre deutliche Präsenz eine der Hauptverantwortungen in der Architektur wahr: die Fokussierung, die Verankerung, dem Umfeld einen Maßstab zu geben.

Das Thema des historischen Stadtkerns, dieses komplexe Zusammenspiel von Bewegung, Aussehen und Abwesenheit, erzeugte den idiomatischen Grundriß für die Stadtbücherei Münster. Das Hengelo Brink Center löst eine ähnlich komplexe urbane Situation durch das Gruppieren von geometrisch strengen Objekten. Bekannte Programme – Passage, Einkaufen, Wohnen (in nicht so vertrauter Form) – werden am existierenden Bahnhof und Marktplatz durch den Elektronischen Campanile und die 120 m lange Passage festgemacht. Die Wohnbebauung an der vorstädtischen Bernhardstraße ist eine Block-Ergänzung, welche auf diesen reagiert, ihn jedoch gleichzeitig neu definiert; sie stellt somit eine weitere Variante dieser mittlerweile vertrauten Verdichtungsstrategie von Bolles+Wilson dar.

In der heutigen Zeit bewegen wir uns in zwei radikal unterschiedlichen und dennoch koexistierenden Stadtmodellen: sowohl in der traditionellen, geographisch fixierten, konzentrischen und in historischen Schichten angelegten europäischen Stadt, als auch in ihrem peripheren Schatten – dem Netzwerk von Infrastruktur und Transport, von außerhalb der Stadt liegenden Einkaufszentren, Brachland, grünen Feldern und von Häusern, die wie Konfetti überall verstreut sind. Diese Eurolandschaft ist mittlerweile überall anzutreffen, ein manchmal sichtbares, aber allgegenwärtiges Netz; sie wird mehr von der Logistik der Warenbewegung und unsichtbarer Informationsflüsse geprägt, als von den festgelegten Formen des traditionellen Planens – eine digitale Patchwork-Landschaft.

Stadtbücherei Münster /
New City Library, 1993

The six recently finished buildings and other projects presented here constitute a second generation of products by the Münster based office of Bolles+Wilson. Post-dating the 1993 opening of the controversial New City Library in Münster, these new works evidence a shift of interests. Particularly in the Warendorfer Straße Office Building, there emerges a new insistence on mass, on the architectural object. The Albeda College in Rotterdam is another such building. Moulded perhaps by the topography and tides of their nebulous context these sharply defined buildings nevertheless through their insistent presence, take up one of the principle responsibilities of architecture: to focus, to anchor, to give measure.

The theme of the Historic Inner City, that complex collaboration of movement, appearance, and absence, generated the idiomatic Münster Library plan. The Hengelo Brink Center resolves a similarly complex urban situation through a grouping of geometrically stringent objects. Familiar programs – passage, shopping, housing (in not so familiar a form) – are pinned and hinged to existing Station and Market Square by the Electronic Campanile and 120m Passage. In the suburbs of Münster, the Bernhardstraße housing, an insertion responding to but at the same time redefining an existing block, is a further use of this now familiar city densifying strategy of Bolles+Wilson.

Today, we occupy on a daily basis two radically different but coexistent city models. The traditional, geographically fixed, concentric, historically layered European city, and its peripheral shadow – that network of infrastructure, transport, out-of-town shopping nodes, wasteland, green fields and a confetti-like sprinkling of housing tracts. This Eurolandschaft has become ubiquitous, a sometimes visible but ever-present network, conditioned more by the logistics of delivery and invisible information flows than the fixed forms of traditional planning – a digital patchwork landscape.

Following Tokyo investigations of the late 1980's, studies into the structural and phenomenological character of this »new Eurolandschaft condition« have formed the background to another type of Bolles+Wilson project. Such contexts require a new vocabulary of architectural response. With the Münster Technology Centre of 1992, the »Iceberg Strategy«

Den Tokio-Untersuchungen des Büros Ende der 80er Jahre folgten Studien zum strukturellen und phänomenologischen Charakter dieses »neuen Eurolandschaft-Zustandes« und bildeten den Hintergrund für eine neue Art von Bolles+Wilson-Projekt. Solche kontextualen Bedingungen erfordern ein neues Vokabular der architektonischen Antwort. 1992 entstand mit dem Technologiehof in Münster die »Eisberg-Strategie«: ein kompakter Solitär, der beinahe willkürlich an seinem Standort »landete«. Seine Größe und seine unbestreitbare Präsenz verankern ihn in dem ansonsten nebulösen Kontext und verleihen diesem wiederum einen Maßstab. Auf städtebaulicher Ebene orchestrierte die 1994er »Hof«-Strategie nicht nur Objekte in einem Feld, sondern die Komposition des Feldes selbst. Die zwei realisierten Projekte im Gewerbepark von Castrop-Rauxel sind ebenfalls typische Eurolandschafts-Ereignisse: Steine, die in ein spektakulär unfokussiertes Feld »geworfen« wurden. Das erste dieser Projekte (DIEZE) strebt mittels Verknüpfung über eine Fußgängerbrücke an den historischen Altstadtkern eine bekannte Art von Urbanität an. Ganz anders das zweite, benachbarte Gebäude, das an irgendeiner beliebigen Stelle »landen« könnte – ein nicht artikuliertes, preiswertes, standardisiertes Fassadensystem. Diese Art von unhierarchischer, nicht spezifizierter Architektur borgt ihre Regeln von der Investitions- und Distributionslogik; das Ergebnis ist ein sehr zeitgenössischer Gebäudetyp – »Box im Feld«.

In Rotterdams Kop van Zuid synthetisieren vier Projekte von Bolles+Wilson die oben genannten Themen. Der »Landing Quay« und der »Rotterdam-Amerika Grenzvorschlag« sind Felder, eine Verstreuung zeichenhafter Elemente auf einem vorbereiteten Boden. Diese Strategie erkennt die potentielle Freiheit der spektakulären, wenn auch nur vorübergehenden Leere des in der Wandlung zur Stadt befindlichen Hafens und macht sie sich zu eigen. Das »Bridgewatcher's House« ist in diesem Fall beides: wiederhergestellte Hafenfunktion und gleichzeitig Wegbereiter einer entstehenden Urbanität. In Zusammenarbeit mit Planungs- und Verkehrsamt haben Bolles+Wilson an dieser Stelle den Fluxus der Stadt zur Orchestrierung des »Landing Square« genutzt und schließlich auch zur »Verankerung« des gesamten Quartiers mit einem Objekt von urbanem Maßstab, einem bedeutsamen kulturellen Fokus – das Neue Luxor Theater.

Technologiehof Münster / Technology Centre 1992

emerged, a compact solitaire landing almost indiscriminately. Its scale and undeniable presence anchoring and again giving measure to its otherwise nebulous context. On an urban planning scale, the 1994 »Hof« strategy orchestrated not only objects, but also the field composition itself. The two realised projects in the Castrop-Rauxel business park are also typical Eurolandschaft events; stones cast in a spectacularly unfocussed field. The first of these (DIEZE) aspires to some familiar sort of urbanity through a connection via a pedestrian bridge to the historic city core. Not so the second and neighbouring building, which could land equally on any site – a non-articulated low cost serialised façade system. Such an unhierarchical, non-specific architecture takes its rules from the logic of investment and distribution; a very contemporary building type – »Box in Field«.

In Rotterdam's Kop van Zuid, four projects by Bolles+Wilson synthesise the above themes. The Landing Quay and the Rotterdam-America border proposal are fields, a scattering of signifiers over a prepared ground. This strategy recognises and appropriates the potential freedom of the evocative, if transitory, emptiness of Harbour in the process of becoming City. The Bridgewatcher's House is here both reinstated harbour function and pioneer of an emerging urbanity. In collaboration with planning and traffic authorities, Bolles+Wilson have here appropriated the flux of the city to orchestrate the Landing Square and, finally, to anchor the whole district with an urban scale object, a major cultural focus – The New Luxor Theatre.

Kräne
Cranes

Einige Berlinexperimente: Forum of Sand 1987: geteiltes Berlin – Kulturforum – Leere; Kronprinzenbrücke 1991: Vereinigung; Bahnhof Spandau 1992: Block und Trajekt; Boxhalle 1993: Urbaner Solitär; Schloß 1994: Wasserforum – Fraktale Wolke; Programme an der Kunsthochschule Weißensee 1993–96: Leere – Masse – Freizeit/Freiheit; Spandau Wasserstadt Nordviertel 1994: Blocks, 1; Spandau Wasserstadt Südspitze 1995: Ein Größerer Block, 2.

in Berlin und Rotterdam

Kann ein Kran eine Stadt repräsentieren? Sicherlich hat ein Skyline-Ballett rotierender Arme Berlin in der Zeit seit der Wiedervereinigung charakterisiert – einen Moment des Übergangs, die Sedimentierung eines stabileren urbanen Zustandes. Es war allerdings in den 20er Jahren schon möglich, daß Vladimir Nabokov (Die Gabe) über den Potsdamer Platz schrieb, er sei »...stets durch Bauarbeiten entstellt«.

Europas größter schwimmender Kran schläft zwischen verschiedenen Aufträgen in Rotterdam, der himmelwärts strebende Arm rivalisiert in seiner Höhe mit den an New York erinnernden Glastürmen, die wie Pilze aus dem Boden schießen. Alain Robbe-Grillet schrieb über eine vergleichbare Stadt (The Erasers): »...dieses Wasser, diese Bewegung hält den Verstand der Menschen offen.«

Berlins Kräne versuchen wieder einmal, die Dinge an ihrem rechten Platz zu richten. Rotterdams Kräne sind Bewegungsapparate, ein ewiges urbanes Schachspiel. Beide Städte befinden sich im Prozeß der Neuerfindung ihrer selbst. Berlin mit seinen Blocks und Blokkierungen, einer Ideologie der Beständigkeit, die – wie in jeder Stadt – von den brennenden Anliegen der Peripherie eingeschränkt wird. Rotterdam, inmitten des logistischen Fluxus der Handelsrouten gelegen und Randstadt, ermutigt offiziell zum Experiment, sowohl im Zentrum als auch in den Docklands – zur Umsetzung der zeitgenössischen Form und zeitgemäßem Programm, urbaner Textur.

Bolles+Wilson befinden sich irgendwo zwischen diesen zwei ideologischen und geographischen Polen. Wir befinden uns selbst oft auf der Reise in beide Richtungen. Was die Realisierung von Projekten betrifft, war Rotterdam die empfänglichere Basis; Berlin ist, vielleicht auf Grund seiner Sturheit, für uns zum Nährboden und Testfeld für Ideen geworden.

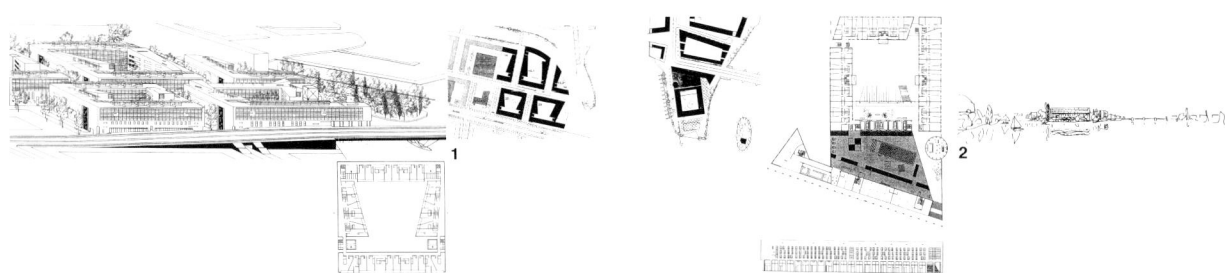

Some Berlin experiments: Forum of Sand 1987: devided Berlin – Culture Forum – Emptiness; Kronprinzen Brücke 1991: Unification; Spandau Station 1992: Block and Trajectory; Boxing Stadium 1993: Urban Solitaire; Schloss 1994: Forum of Water – Fractal Cloud; Programs Kunsthochschule Weissensee 1993–96: Emptiness – Mass – Free Time/ Freedom; Spandau Wasserstadt Nordviertel 1994: Blocks, 1; Spandau Wasserstadt Südspitze 1995: a Bigger Block, 2.

in Berlin and Rotterdam

Can a crane represent a city? Certainly a skyline ballet of rotating arms has characterised post unification Berlin; a moment of transition, the sedimentation of a more stable urban state. It was also possible in the 1920's, though, for Vladimir Nabokov (The Gift) to write of a Potsdamer Platz »...always disfigured by city works«.

Europe's largest floating crane sleeps between jobs in Rotterdam. Its soaring arm rivalling in height the mushrooming New York-like glass towers. As Alain Robbe-Grillet wrote of a similar city (The Erasers), »...this water, this movement keeps people's minds open.«

Berlin's cranes are trying once again to fix things in their right place. Rotterdam´s are instruments of movement, a perpetual urban chess game. These are both cities in the process of reinventing themselves. Berlin, with its blocks and blockages, is an ideology of permanence circumscribed by, as in every city, the burning issues of the periphery. Rotterdam, located in the logistic flux of trade routes and Randstadt, is officially encouraging experiment in both Center and Docklands; the implementation of contemporary form and program, urban texture.

Bolles+Wilson are located somewhere between these two ideological and geographical poles. We often find ourselves travelling in both directions. In terms of realisation, Rotterdam has been the most receptive and perhaps because of its resistance Berlin has assumed for us the status of laboratory.

Masse im Medienzeitalter
Mass in the Age of Media

Der gegenwärtige Status eines Architekturwerkes muß vor dem Hintergrund der heutigen technologischen und wahrnehmungstechnischen Möglichkeiten bestimmt werden. Elektronisch übermittelte Information, wie Walter Benjamins »mechanische Reproduktion« rekonstituiert nicht nur das Sichtbare und Verfahrenstechnische, sondern auch unser Verhältnis zu Zeit und Material. Das Digitale überschattet heutzutage das Topographische, das Virtuelle verdrängt das Physische. Abgesehen von der täglich voranschreitenden Revolutionierung ihrer Produktionsprozesse, scheint es nun der Architektur (im Gefolge der Medien) möglich zu werden, lästige Materialität zu Gunsten von verführerischer, letztlich jedoch unzugänglicher Virtualität aufzugeben. Diese Option lehnen wir ab.

Die Frage ist: Kann und soll Architektur die gleichen Qualitäten, die unserer neu erworbenen Sensibilität zu eigen sind (Transparenz, Unbeständigkeit), vermitteln? Dies wäre ein der Aneignung und Ästhetisierung industrieller Formen und utilitaristischer Prinzipien durch den Modernismus des frühen zwanzigsten Jahrhunderts vergleichbarer Wandel. Der Vergleich »Haus/Maschine« ist plausibel, denn beide verbindet eine relativ ähnliche Maßstäblichkeit und Langlebigkeit. Ein Vergleich »CD-ROM/Gebäude« ist allerdings eine vollkommen andere Frage.

Welche Qualitäten haben das Gebaute und das Digitale gemeinsam? Die Oberfläche: Monitor und Fassade, beide Flächen für Inschriften, die eine mit virtueller Tiefe, die andere mit materieller Tiefe. Als Informationsträger (post-Gutenberg/post-TV) hat Architektur die Rolle eines stillen Beobachters eingenommen. Nicht mehr lesbar (als Buch oder Menü), kann sie nicht via Satellit zu irgend einem Punkt auf dem Globus gebeamt werden; Architektur kann als Informationsträger mit der phänomenalen Kapazität von Software einfach nicht konkurrieren.

Also liegen die Qualitäten von Architektur anderswo – in ihrer Beständigkeit, ihrer konkreten und haptischen Präsenz, ihrer Umrahmung des alltäglichen Lebens. Im Hinblick auf

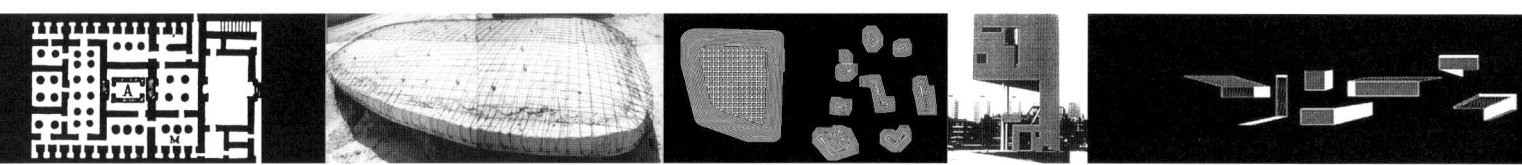

The current status of a work of architecture must be measured against the background of today's technological and perceptual possibilities. Electronically conveyed information, like Walter Benjamin´s mechanical reproduction, re-constitutes not only the visible and the procedural, but also our relation to time and material. Today, the digital overshadows the topographical, the virtual »de-presences« the physical. Besides the everyday revolutionising of its production processes, there now seems for architecture (in the wake of media) the possibility to abandon troublesome materiality in favour of a seductive but ultimately inaccessible virtual reality. This option we reject.

The question is whether architecture can or should convey the same qualities endemic to our new mediated sensibility (transparency, impermanence) – a transference comparable to the appropriation and aestheticising of industrial forms and utilitarian principles by early twentieth century modernism. A house/machine comparison is plausible; they share a relatively similar scale and duration. A CD-ROM/building comparison is quite another question.

What qualities do the built and the digital have in common? Surface – monitor and façade: both are surfaces of inscription, one with virtual depth, one with material depth. As a carrier of information (post Gutenberg, post TV), architecture has become a silent bystander. No longer read (like a book or menu), it cannot be beamed by satellite to any point on the globe. It simply cannot compete as an information carrier against the phenomenal capacity of digital data.

The qualities of architecture lie elsewhere: its duration, its concrete and haptic presence, its framing of everyday life. In terms of duration media is instantaneous. Buildings on the other hand, after their protracted and laborious incubation and realisation, »stay«. We get to know them slowly, through the habits of use.

In their »staying«, buildings become their place, their site. Such singular locations are just as unrepeatable as transmitted information is ubiquitous and simultaneous.

Dauer sind Medien unmittelbar. Nach ihrer langwierigen und mühsamen Inkubation und Ausführung bleiben Gebäude hingegen »da«. Wir lernen sie langsam kennen, durch die Gewohnheiten des Gebrauchs.

Durch ihr »Da-Bleiben« werden Gebäude zu ihrem Platz, ihrem eigenen Ort. Diese einzigartigen Orte sind so unwiederholbar, wie teletransportierte Informationen allgegenwärtig und simultan sind.

Die Medien erreichen uns überall, zur Architektur müssen wir hingehen. Die Medienfassade, der Architektur neue Kleider, ist in diesem Sinne anachronistisch, ein Hybrid. Als Spektakel im traditionellen Sinn fordert sie die unmittelbare Nähe ihres Publikums. Aber das Feld der sozialen Interaktion ist nicht länger ortsspezifisch, TV und Internet sind die Piazzas von heute.

Architektur setzt den Maßstab für ihren unmittelbaren Kontext und für das Kommen und Gehen der täglichen Nutzung. Sie kann niemals ganz vom Maßstab, dem Eindruck des menschlichen Körpers getrennt werden. Andererseits resultieren die schwindelerregenden fraktalen Permutationen der Mediennetzwerke in der Un-Tiefe, der gleichen Nähe und nichtssagenden Fadheit von 24-Stunden-Nachrichten. Eine solche Un-Tiefe scheint auch unsere unendlich durchlässigen und banalen post-urbanen Siedlungsmuster zu charakterisieren.

Letztlich ist es ihre Masse, welche die Architektur am meisten von den flüchtigen Bildern der elektronischen Medien unterscheidet. Das Veranschaulichen von Masse führt zu einer Eduardo-Chilida-ähnlichen Formensprache – einem soliden homogenen Volumen, das innerhalb der materiellen Grenzen seiner körperlichen Integrität moduliert ist. Masse in der Architektur spricht von einer Solidität, die impliziert, aber nicht wörtlich zu verstehen ist – wie bei Kühltürmen, deren äußere Massivität die vollständige Leere ihres Inneren und damit ihre eigentliche Funktion ermöglicht (den effizienten Luftstrom). Der Technologiehof in Münster, 1992 von Bolles+Wilson entworfen, nutzte diese Art von scheinbarer Masse, um einen ansonsten nebulösen Kontext zu fokussieren und zu verankern. In dem heute teppichähnlichen urbanen Feld (dem physischen Ergebnis der Unbestimmbarkeit der Logistik) kann Architektur nicht länger hoffen, das Ganze ordnen zu können (was die Ambition

Media comes to us (anywhere); we go to architecture. The media façade – architecture's new clothes – is in this sense anachronistic, a hybrid. A spectacle in the traditional sense, it demands the close proximity of its audience. But the field of social interaction is no longer place specific. Television and the Internet are today's piazzas.

Architecture gives measure to its immediate context, to the comings and goings of daily use. It can never be totally disconnected from the scale and imprint of the human body. The

dizzying fractal permutations of media networks, on the other hand, result in the non-depth, the equal nearness and the blandness of 24-hour news. Such a depth also seems to characterise our infinitely permeable, and infinitely forgettable, post-urban settlement patterns.

Ultimately, it is mass which most distinguishes architecture from the fleeting images of electronic media. Exemplifying mass leads towards an Eduardo Chillida-like form language – a solid homogenous volume modulated within the material limits of its corporal integrity. In architecture, mass speaks of a solidity that is implied but not literal. Like cooling towers, where the external massiveness facilitates the complete voiding of the interior, an allowing of its function (the efficient flow of air). Bolles+Wilson's 1992 Technology Center in Münster used such an apparent mass to focus and anchor an otherwise nebulous peripheral context. In today's carpet-like urban field (the physical consequence of the indeterminacy of logistics), architecture can no longer hope to bring order to the whole (the ambition of nineteenth century planning). Instead, by focussing its unambiguous presence, its mass, architecture has the possibility to hold fast, to anchor and to give measure to the surrounding flux. The »iceberg strategy« – mass in the age of media.

At the level of detail – and on the level of phenomenological experience – the perseverance of mass and the haptic quality of material surface is today a necessary counterpoint to the dematerialised projections of cinema, video and media. It is now more consequent for architecture to »stay«, not to chase chimerical electronic shadows, but to insist on the necessity and clarity of its mass.

der Städteplanung im neunzehnten Jahrhundert war). Stattdessen hat Architektur durch ihre eindeutige Präsenz, ihre Masse und ihr Fokussieren die Möglichkeit festzuhalten, zu verankern, dem umgebenden Fluxus einen Maßstab zu verleihen. – Die »Eisberg-Strategie«: Masse im Medienzeitalter.

Auf der Ebene des Details – und jener der phänomenologischen Erfahrung – setzen die Beharrlichkeit der Masse und die haptische Qualität der Materialoberfläche einen notwen-

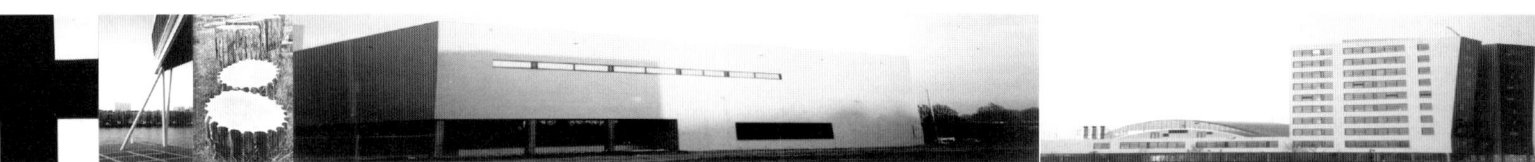

digen Kontrapunkt zu den entmaterialisierten Projektionen von Kino, Video und Medien. Heutzutage ist es für die Architektur konsequenter, »da zu bleiben« und auf der Notwendigkeit und Klarheit ihrer Masse zu bestehen – anstatt trügerische, elektronische Schatten zu jagen.

Bürogebäude WLV
Office Building WLV

Bauherr/Client: WLV
Westfälisch-Lippische
Vermögensverwal-
tungsgesellschaft mbH
Standort/Location:
Warendorfer Straße,
Münster
Fertigstellung/
Completion: 1995
Projektassistent/
Project Assistant:
Martin Schlüter
Statiker/Structural
Engineer: Gantert-
Ingenieur-Planung
Techniker/Technician:
Werning & Dr.
Schmickler

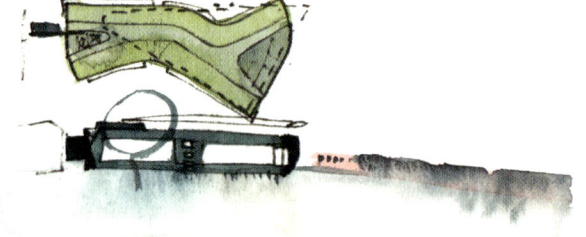

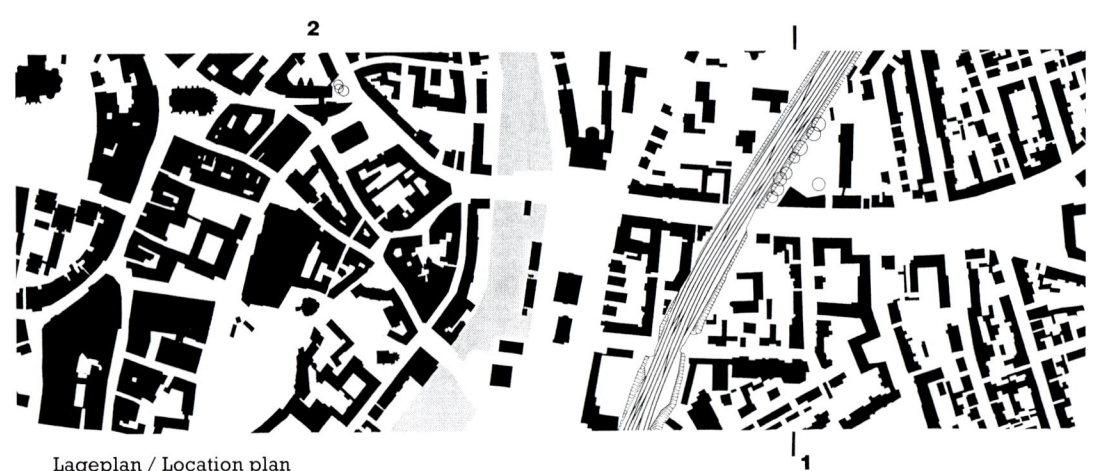

Lageplan / Location plan
1 Bürogebäude WLV / Office Building WLV
2 Stadtbücherei / City Library

Bahndamm-Ecke / Corner to tracks

Programm
Ein einfaches, kompaktes Verwaltungsgebäude mit 3 Bürogeschossen (1,625 m Fenster- und Planungsraster), Läden auf Straßenniveau, Kantine/Restaurant im Dachgeschoß.

Program
A straightforward administration building, three floors of office (1.625 m planning axis), shops at street level, restaurant on the roof.

Dachgeschoß – Kantine
Roof – Canteen

3. OG – Büros und Konferenzräume
3rd floor – Offices and conference rooms

1./2. OG – Büros
1st/2nd floor – Offices

EG – Geschäfte
Ground floor – Shops

UG – Neben-/Ausbildungsräume
Basement – Service/Seminar rooms

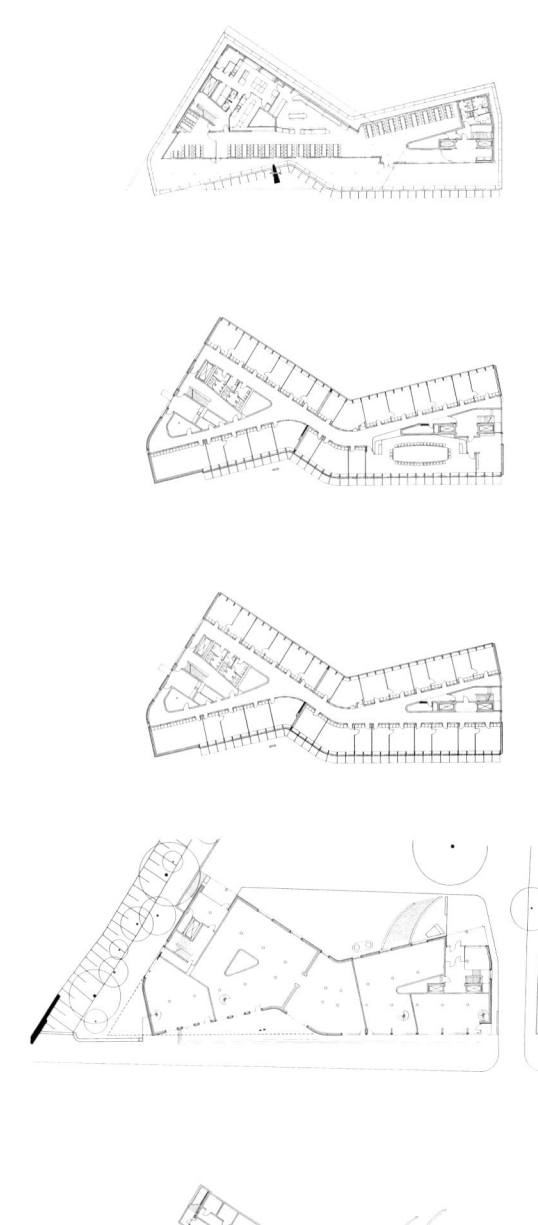

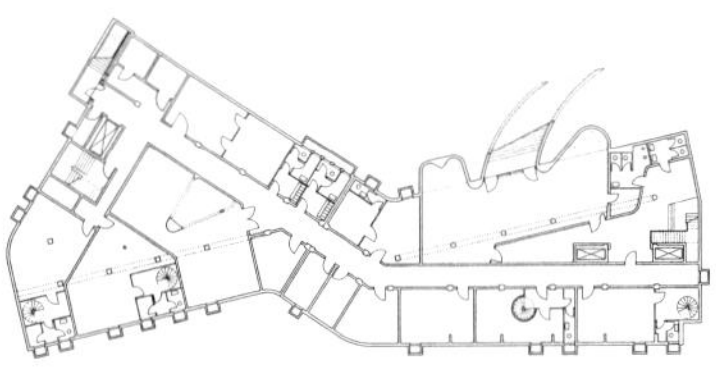

Flur und Service-Insel / Passage and service Island

$x^2 x^3$. Elastischer Plan

Vorgegebene lineare Bürostreifen, zusammen mit den Abweichungen aus dem Kontext, produzieren den elastischen Plan. Der elastische Plan springt im Grundriß von der Zwei- zur Dreibündigkeit. Der elastische Plan belebt standardisierte Büroräume, eliminiert monotone Korridore, erzeugt interessante Sonderräume an den Richtungswechseln. Er ist gleichzeitig konstruktiv optimal.

$x^2 x^3$ The elastic plan

Given linear office strips plus contextual deflections produce the Elastic Plan. The Elastic Plan springs from double to triple layered office planning. The Elastic Plan animates serialised offices, elevates monotonous corridors, and creates interesting hinge rooms. It is, at the same time, constructionally optimal.

Aus dem Preisgerichtsprotokoll

Die Bürogeschosse sind als zweibündige Anlage entwickelt, wobei die überzeugende Position der Erschließungs- und Versorgungskerne an den problematischen Stirnseiten (Bahnlärm/Licht) zu einer spielerischen Aufweitung und Aufspaltung der Korridore führt.

From the jury report

A regular office layout of passage with office on both sides is animated by the location of stairs and service rooms at the problematic short sides of the building (train noise, light). These two islands create a playful and lively internal landscape.

Straße und Bahnüberführung von der Dachterrasse
Street and railway bridge from the roof terrace

Bleimodell / Lead model

22 BÜROGEBÄUDE

Süd-Ansicht / South elevation

Masse
Seit dem original aus Blei gegossenen Wettbewerbsmodell ist das Thema dieses Gebäudes seine körperliche Integrität, seine präzise Darstellung, seine Masse. Aus der Nähe wird diese einzelne Form als eine sinnliche Oberfläche erlebt. Das Flaschengrün der glasierten Ziegel wurde speziell entwikkelt. Im Schatten erscheint es schwarz. Durch seine reflektierende Qualität kann es auch den Glanz des Himmels annehmen.
Ein Gebäude, das lebt.

Mass
Since the original lead-cast competition model, the subject of this building has been its corporal integrity, its precise delineation, its mass. Close up, this single form is experienced as a sensual surface. The bottle green of the glazed brick was specially developed. In shadow it appears black. Through its reflective quality, it can also take on the brilliance of the sky.
A building that lives.

Dachflügel / Roofwing

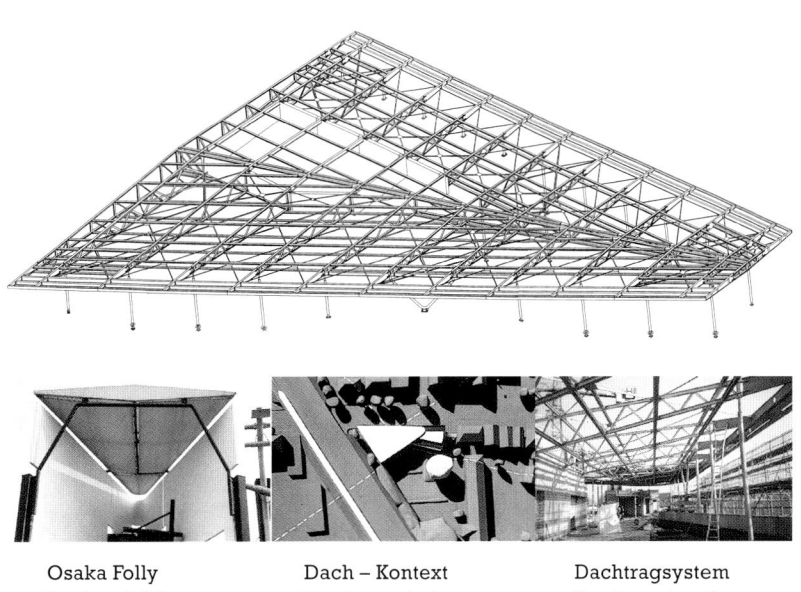

Osaka Folly	Dach – Kontext	Dachtragsystem
Dachvorbild	Roof – context	Roof construction
Roof principle		

25　OFFICE BUILDING

Nordfassade mit Innenhof / Northfaçade to courtyard

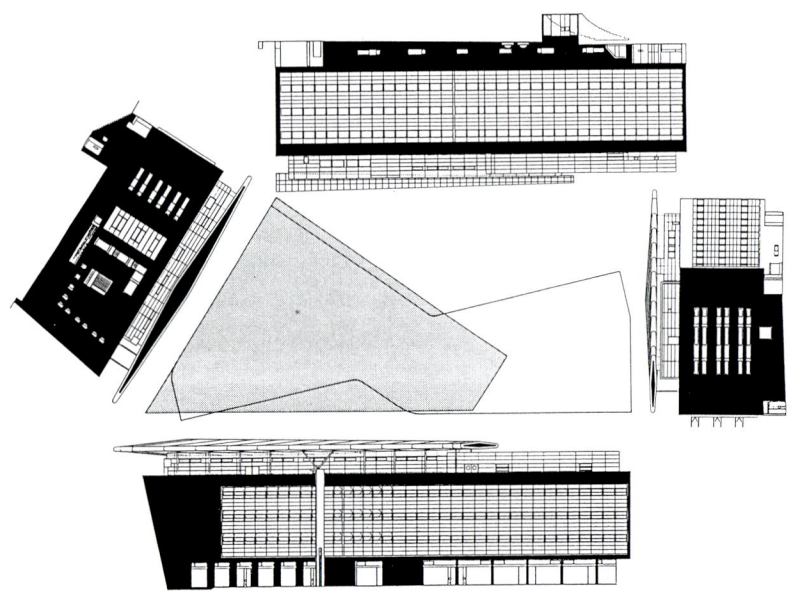

Ansichten / Elevation projections

26 BÜROGEBÄUDE

Büroeingang / Office entrance

Haltepunkte

Für den Bahnreisenden ist die grüne (glasierte Ziegel-) Box ein Ereignis, das nur Sekunden andauert, ihre Einbuchtungen vielleicht nur ein Effekt der Geschwindigkeit, ihr Dach schwebt vielleicht nur einen Augenblick lang. Für den Autofahrer und Fußgänger, deren tägliches Passieren ihr architektonisches Äquivalent in den horizontalen Sonnenschutzstreifen der Fassade findet, wird das Gebäude allmählich zum sedimentierten und integralen Bestandteil der Straße – ein Haltepunkt, eine Insel, ein fixiertes Objekt, an dem die Stadt gemessen werden kann.

Stoppage

For the train traveller, the green (glazed brick) box is an event of a few seconds duration, its deflections perhaps only the effect of speed, its roof perhaps only temporarily hovering. For commuter and pedestrians whose daily passings find their architectural equivalent in the façade's sun louver stripes, the building will gradually sediment, become part of the street; a stoppage, an island, a fixed object against which the city can be measured.

Zurückweichende Flurwand / Twisting passage wall

Sonnenlamellen / Sun screens

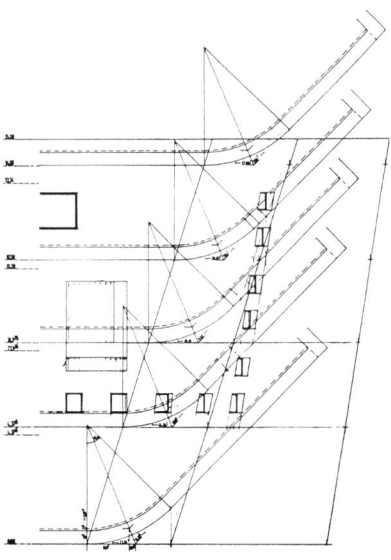
Kurven-Geometrie / Curve geometry

BÜROGEBÄUDE

Abgetrepptes Mauerwerk / Corbelled wall

Abweichungen
Eine radiale Einkaufsstraße wird knapp außerhalb der historischen Stadtgrenze Münsters gekreuzt von der Haupt-Nord-Süd-Bahnverbindung (Zürich nach Kopenhagen), eine Kollision zweier Geschwindigkeiten, ganz unterschiedlicher räumlicher Typen, Korridore von lokaler und ausgedehnter Bewegung. Eine alltägliche Kollision, nicht ausreichend, um das Gebäude als Objekt zu zerstören, jedoch stark genug, um die Fassadenlinie zu verbiegen. Die Straße dreht sich in sich selbst zurück und der Raum dahinter wird eingerahmt.

Deflections
A radial shopping street is crossed just outside the historic city boundary by the main, north- south railway line (Zurich to Copenhagen); a collision of two speeds, of two distinct spatial types, corridors of local and extended movement.
An everyday sort of collision, not enough to disintegrate the building-as-object, but sufficient to deflect façade lines.
The street turns back on itself; a space behind is framed.

Kurve
Nur einmal weicht die Grundform von der Vertikalen ab (durch den Kontext verursacht). In der Kurve der Westfassade weicht jeder Ziegel 1 cm von seinem stützenden Kurs ab. Die Haut fließt von der Vertikalen in eine Schräge. Ein einfacher Kunstgriff, der auf die Genauigkeit des Maurerhandwerks angewiesen ist, um seinen Effekt zu erhalten – Masse wird formbar.

Curve
Only once does the principle form diverge from the vertical (site induced). Within the curve of the west façade, each brick course slips 1 cm from its supporting course. The skin flows from vertical to sloped. A simple device which relies on the skill of the craftsman bricklayers for its effect – mass made plastic.

Treppe / Stair detail

Eingangshalle / Entrance hall

31 OFFICE BUILDING

Das Gebäude ist als Stahlbetonskelettbau errichtet, mit einer hinterlüfteten Klinkerfassade. Die Fensterprofile sind silbermetallisch, ebenso der feststehende Sonnenschutz aus Gitterrosten, der außerordentlich wirkungsvoll beschattet, ohne die Transparenz der Fassade von innen oder außen einzuschränken.

> The building is constructed from in situ and pre-cast concrete elements with a hung brick façade. Windows and sunscreens are metallic silver. The south façade is fully shaded without reducing internal or external transparency.

Büroprinzip
Das Gebäude wurde auf einer 1,625 m großen Achsenmasse geplant. Die vorgefertigten tragenden Betonelemente bilden auf jeder Achse eine 65 cm tiefe Fensterzone für alle notwendigen Büroversorgungen (Kabelkanal, Heizung, Blumen-/Fensterbank, Sonnenschutz). Die Fensterprofile verschwinden hinter diesen Scheiben
(Masse = Transparenz).

> ### Office principle
> The building is planned on a 1,625-m module. Pre-cast concrete fins (exposed structure) on every axis provide a 65 cm deep window zone for all necessary office servicing (cable canal, heating, flower shelf, glare shield). Window profiles disappear behind these fins
> (mass = transparency).

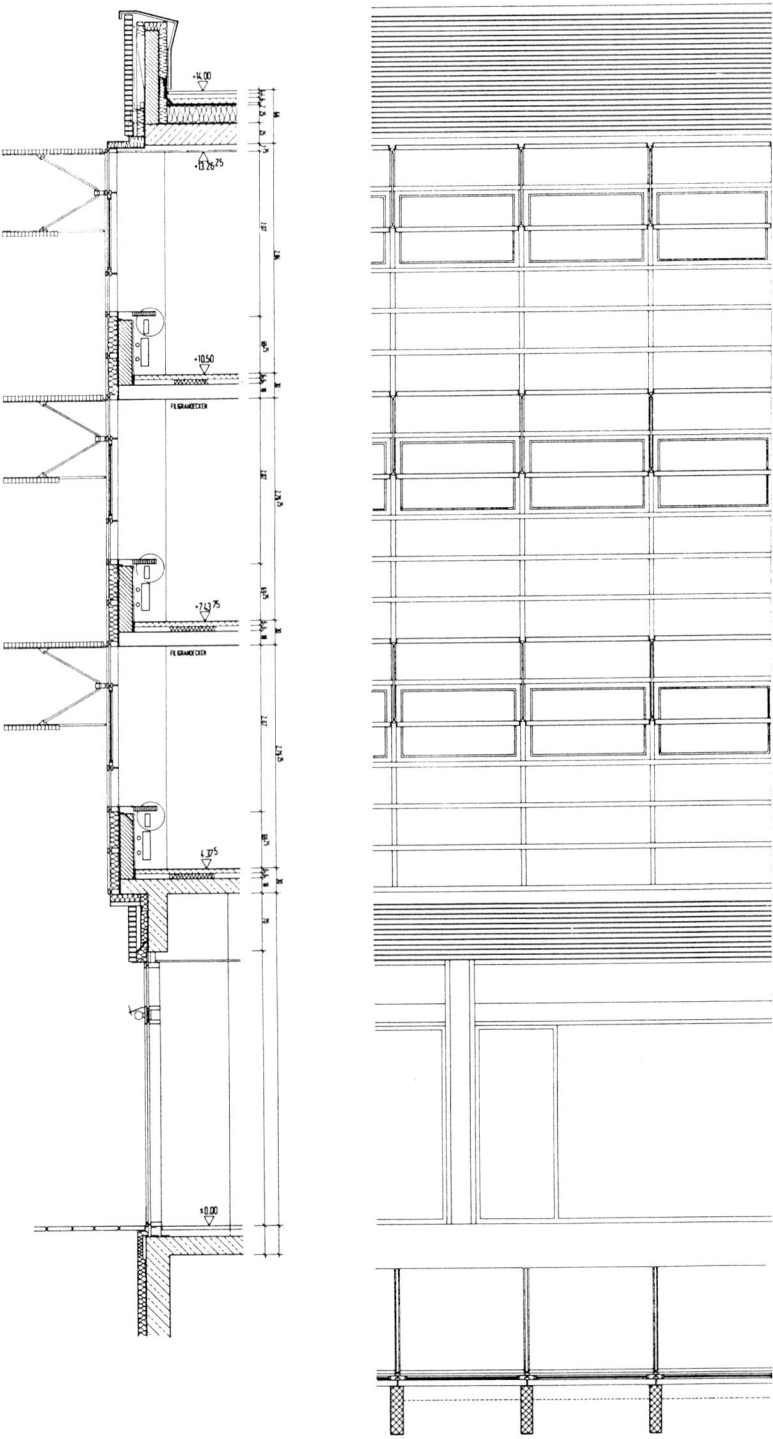

Tragende Betonfertigteile als Büroelement /
Supporting precast fins as office element

Büroschrankwand / Office wall system

33 OFFICE BUILDING

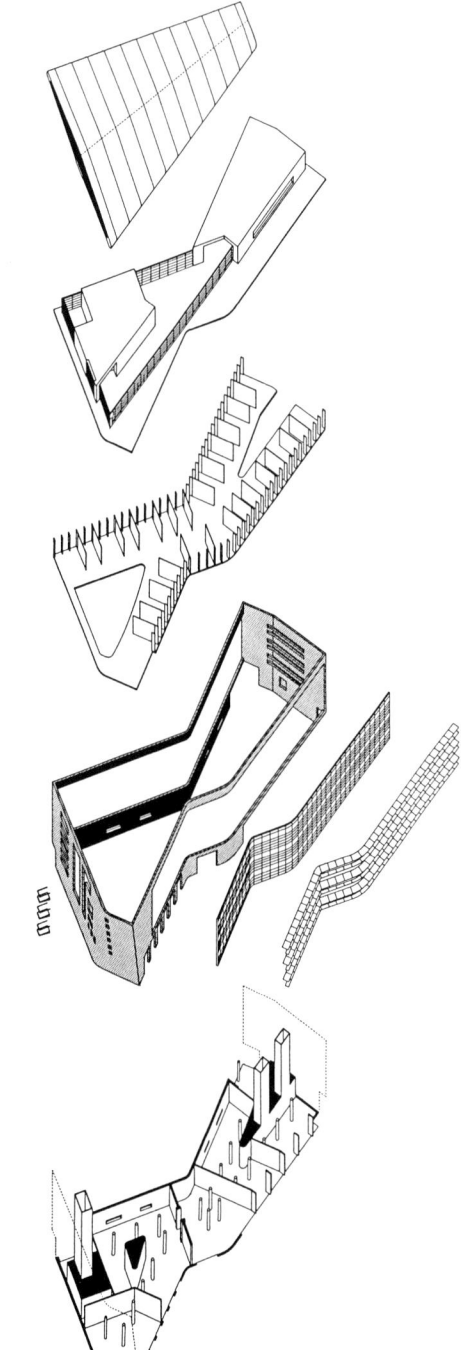

Dach / Roof

Kantine / Canteen

Büros / Offices

Fassade und Lamellen
Façade and sun screens

EG Geschäfte / Ground floor shops

Haupttreppe / Office main stairway

Konferenzraum Garderobe
Conference room coat and hat stand

Konferenztisch für 38 Personen / 38 Seater
Rechts: Schallwand, links: Betonrippen /
Right: acoustic wall, left: concrete fins

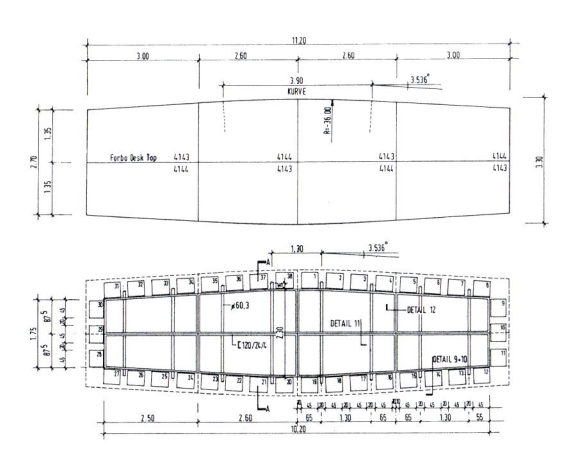

37   OFFICE BUILDING

Kantine und Dach / Canteen and roof

Kantineneingang / Canteen entrance

Kantine – Innenstadt-Ausblick / Canteen – city outlook

Aus dem Preisgerichtsprotokoll
Die Kantine nutzt die bevorzugte Lage auf dem Dach. Die Raumkante bleibt hinter der Brüstung zurück, so daß eine Aussichtsterrasse zur Innenstadt entsteht, die durch den Dachflügel geschützt ist.

From the jury report
The rooftop canteen stays behind the façade line and is protected by the »roofwing«, allowing a terrace with spectacular views of the inner city.

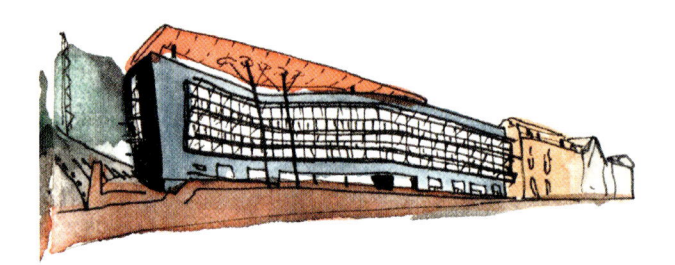

Wettbewerbsskizze / Competition sketch

Kantine: Trennwand mit Rollo / Canteen: dividing wall with roll blinds
Rechts: Seminarraum Oberlichter / Right: seminar room skylights

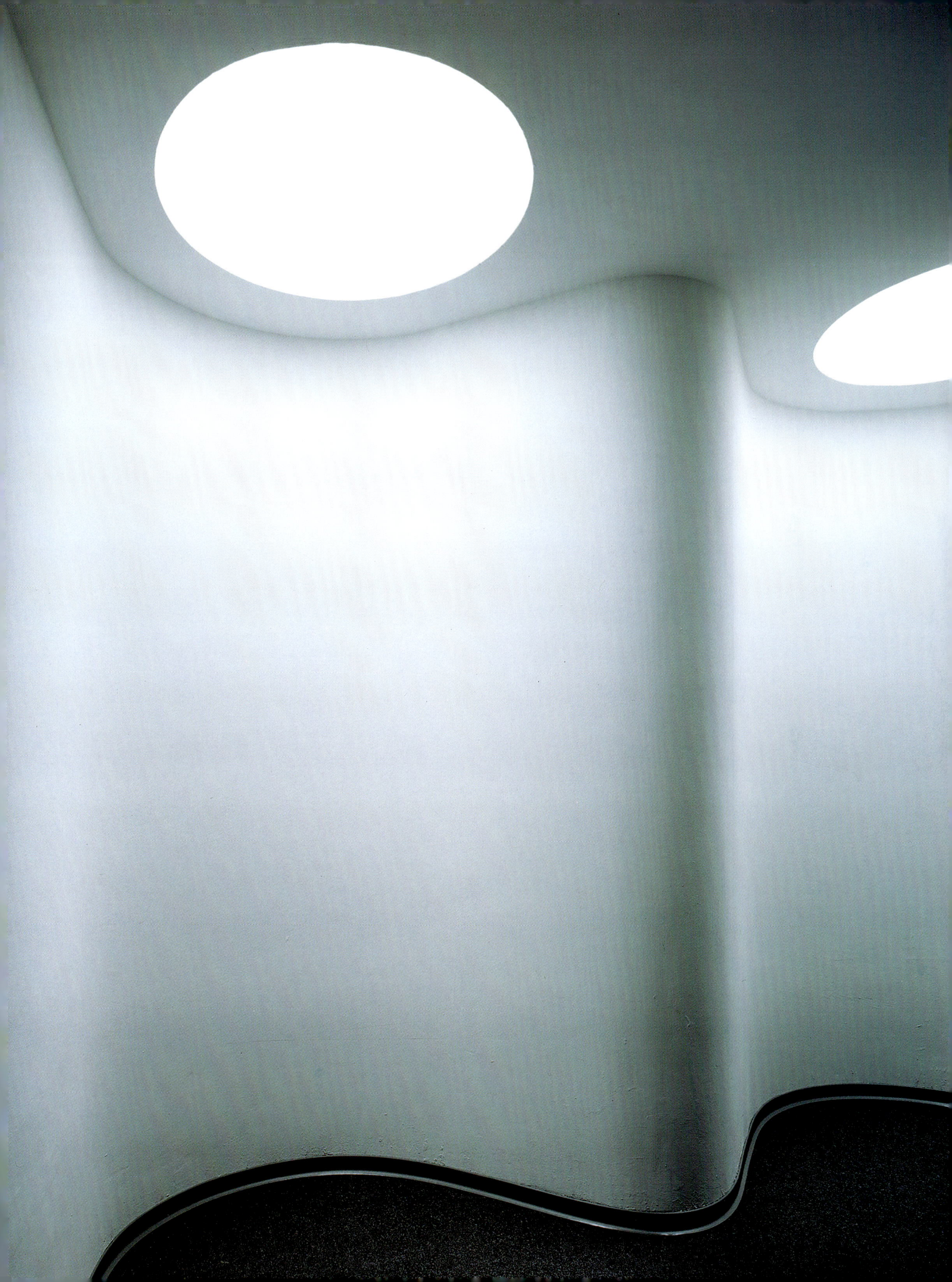

Kundenzentrum Zumtobel/Staff
Customer Centre Zumtobel/Staff

Bauherr/Client:
Zumtobel / Staff GmbH
& Co. KG
Standort/Location:
Grevenmarschstraße,
Lemgo
Fertigstellung/
Completion: 1996
Projektassistent/
Project Assistant:
Jim Yohe
Lichtdesign/Lighting
Design: AG Licht, Köln

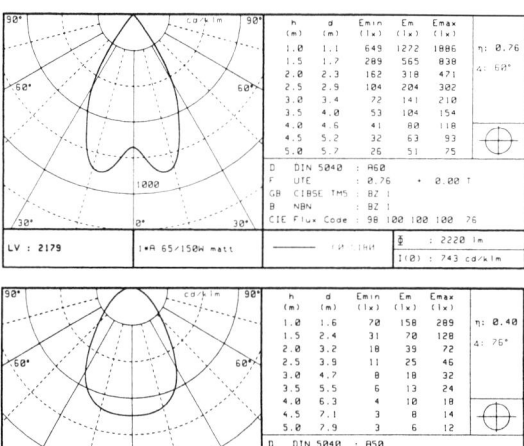

Grundriß Konzept / Plan concept

Errichtung eines neuen Kundenzentrums für ZUMTOBEL/STAFF auf 1.000 qm einer bestehenden Produktionshalle. Der Fußboden der flexiblen Demonstrationshalle zeigt ein cd/klm Diagramm mit konzentrischen Winkelkreisen. Einziger Fixpunkt in der Halle ist der Konferenzraum in Form einer Lichtverteilungskurve. Ein verblüffend einfaches Image – Gebautes Licht.

A new Customer Centre for the lighting firm Zumtobel/Staff in an existing 1,000-m^2 industrial shed. The large scale, flexible demonstration hall has a cd/klm – light distribution diagram imprinted on the floor. The one fixed point is a particular light curve projected vertically as the walls of an enclosed conference room. This simple translation leads directly to the elegant conference room form and to the title – Built Light.

Lageplan / Site

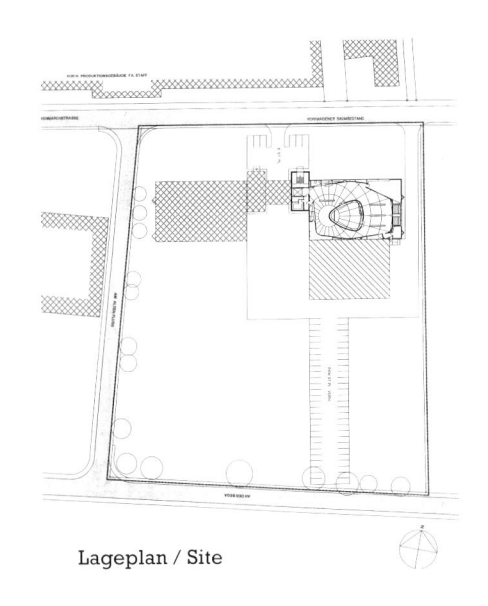

Eingang / Entrance Cloud

Boden / Floor   Decke / Ceiling

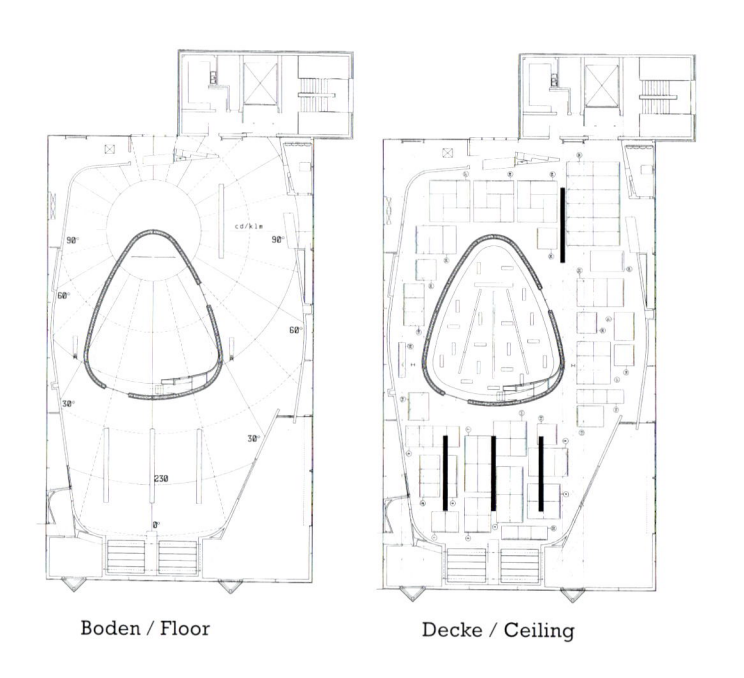

Konferenzsaal / Conference room

44   KUNDENZENTRUM

Dolmetscherkabine / Translator's cabin

Der mit Kirschbaumfurnier ausgekleidete Konferenzraum faßt zwischen 45 und 80 Personen, je nach Möblierung. Er kann für Konferenzen, Seminare und Vorträge genutzt werden. Seine Wände werden durch Licht von Boden und Decke getrennt.
Die Halle wird nach innen durch eine neue, vollkommen weiße Wand konturiert, die Zweite Haut. Zwischen dieser und der bestehenden Außenwand sind kleinere Räume mit sehr spezifischem Lichtambiente untergebracht: Empfang, Büro, Besprechungsräume, Kundenberatung, Cafeteria.

The cherry-wood clad conference room seats between 45 and 80, for conference, seminar or lecture. Its walls are separated by light from floor and ceiling.
The hall itself is wrapped by a new white plasterboard screen (second skin) – the register for various light qualities. Sandwiched between this and the containing box are smaller rooms, each with its own light ambience (reception, design office, meeting rooms, bar, storage).

Cloud, Skin, Blob

Das schwarz gespritzte Trägersystem der Decke erlaubt die flexible Versuchsanordnung von abgehängten Deckenfeldern mit eingebauten oder abgependelten Leuchten: Technical Clouds. Decke und Wand erlauben vielfältige räumliche Simulationen und Leuchtenanordnungen. Für die technische und experimentelle Demonstration gibt es zwei nischenartige Workshops, in denen durch bewegliche Decken unterschiedliche räumliche Situationen simuliert werden können. Zusätzlich gibt es fahrbare Wagen und Paneele. Mit diesen läßt sich in der Halle eine variable Ausstellungslandschaft für Raum- und Lichtsimulierung bauen sowie für die Demonstration der Leuchten und ihres Einbaus im Detail, sozusagen zum Anfassen.

> From existing blacked out ceiling trusses hang a geometric constellation of Technical Clouds – exchangeable fields of built in or hung lights – the actual displayed products. This variable ceiling in combination with free standing display walls allow a great variety of spatial simulations for experimental demonstration. Two niche-like workshops with lowerable ceilings facilitate more technical demonstration. The choreography of the exhibition landscape is activated by a series of roving-exhibition furniture also as many of the light demonstration assemblies by Bolles + Wilson.

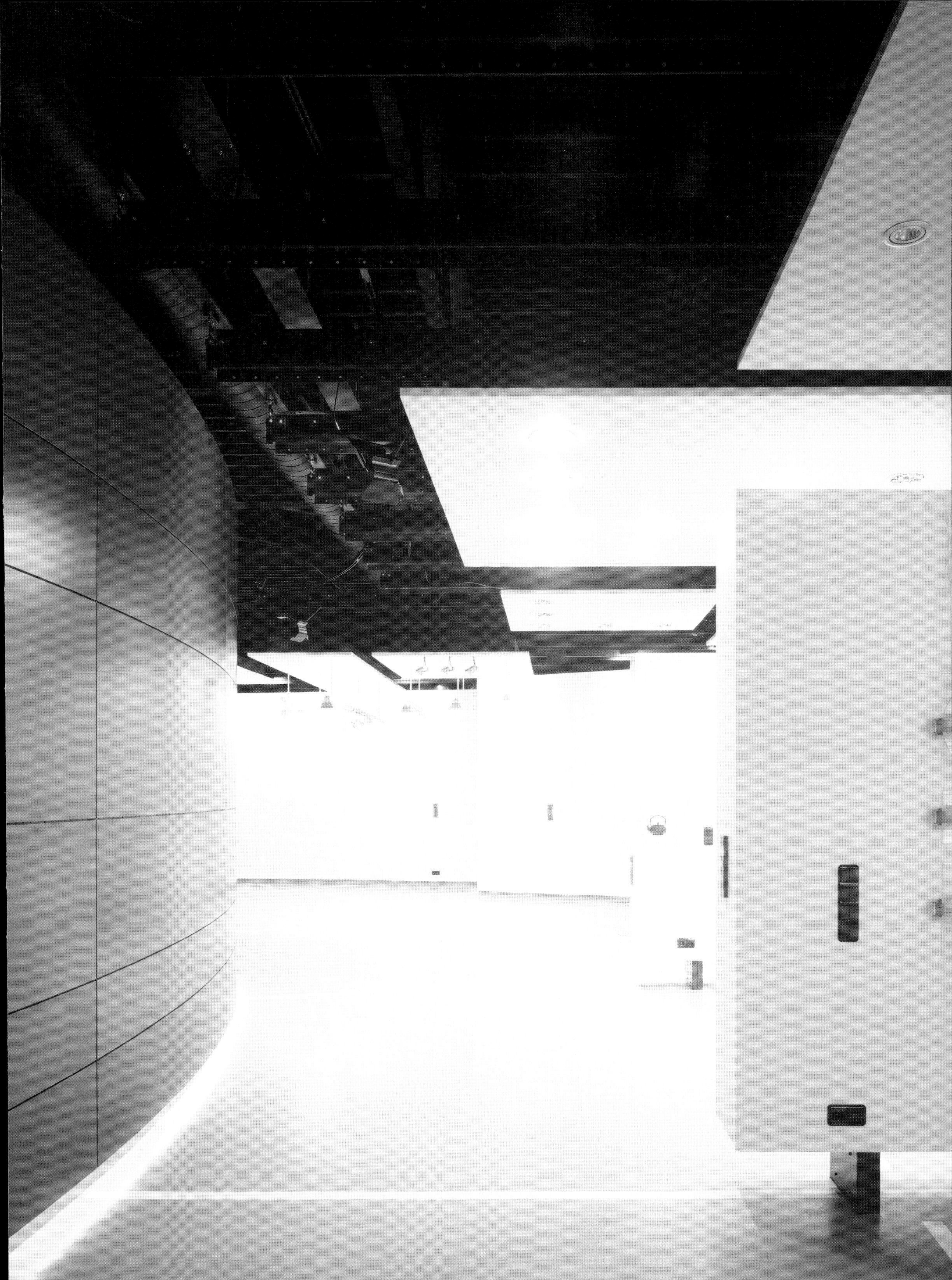

Lichttragende Wand / Light carrying wall

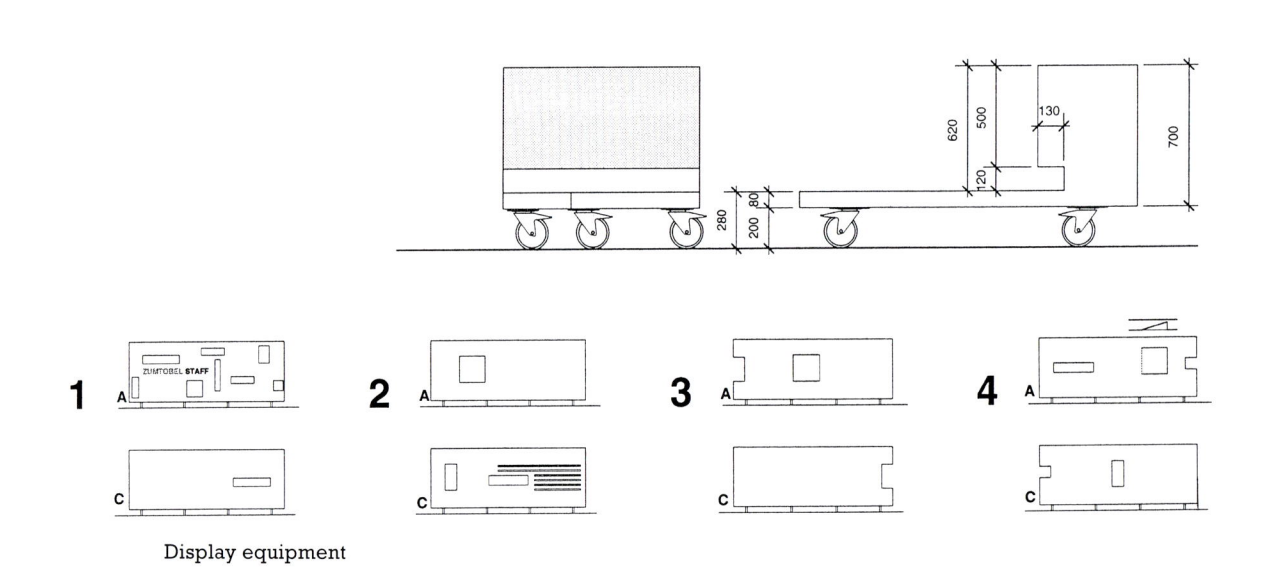

1   2   3   4

Display equipment

48 KUNDENZENTRUM

Lichtlandschaft / Light landscape

Verwaltungsgebäude WLV
Administration Building WLV

Bauherr/Client: WLV
Westfälisch-Lippische
Vermögensverwal-
tungsgesellschaft mbH
Standort/Location:
Zumsandestraße,
Münster
Fertigstellung/
Completion: 1999
Projektassistent/
Project Assistant:
Jürgen Zils
Statiker/Structural
Engineer: Gantert-
Ingenieur-Planung
Techniker/Technician:
Winkels & Behrens

**WLV, 2. Verwaltungsgebäude,
Zumsandestraße Münster**
Blockverdichtung, ein Maßstabssprung vom
Wohnen zum Verwaltungsgebäude des 19.
Jahrhunderts. Ein neuer Platz. Ein Fahrradweg,
durch die Textur der Stadt gewebt, eine
formale Komplexität erzeugend, ein Ereignis
im urbanen Plan, eine Unterbrechung.

**WLV, 2nd Administration Building,
Zumsandestraße Münster**
Block infill, a scale jump from housing to
nineteenth century administration edifice.
A new square. A bicycle route woven
through the fabric of the city precipitating
a formal complexity, an event in the urban
plan, a »stoppage«.

WLV 1

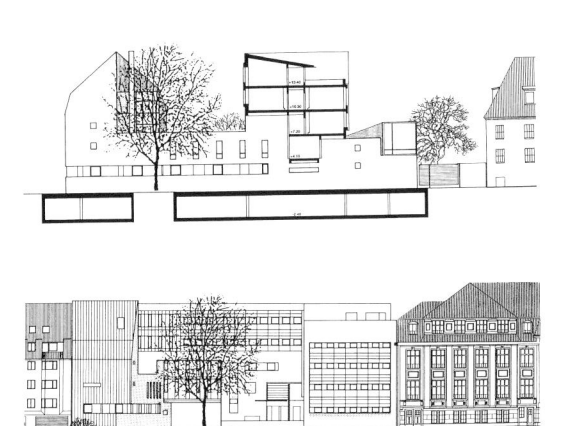

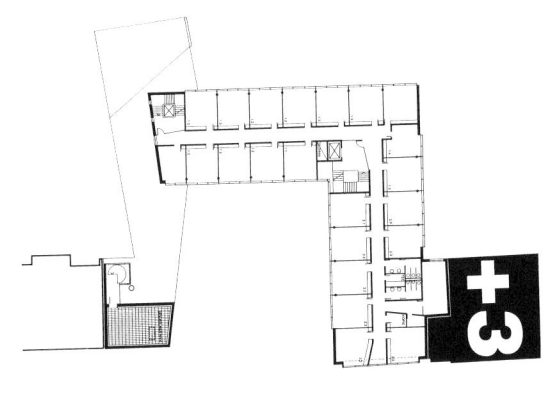

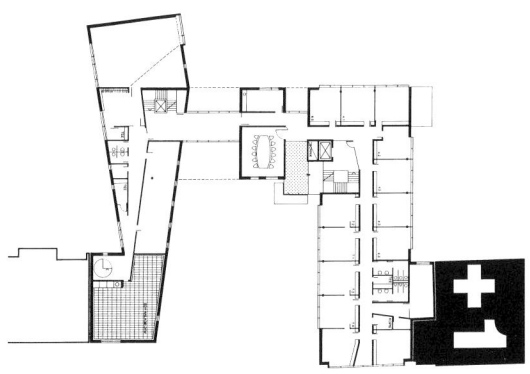

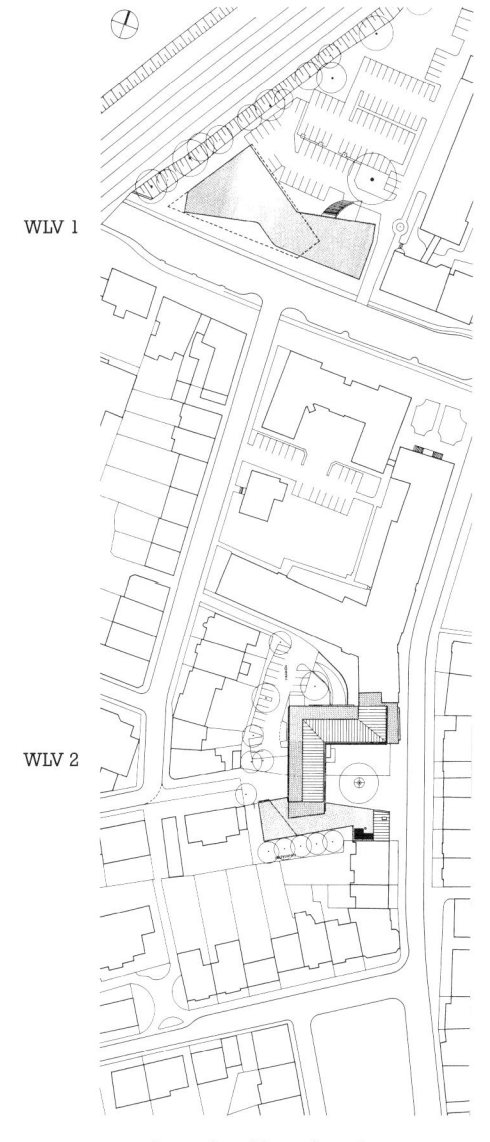

WLV 2

Lageplan / Location plan

Wohnprojekte
Residential Projects

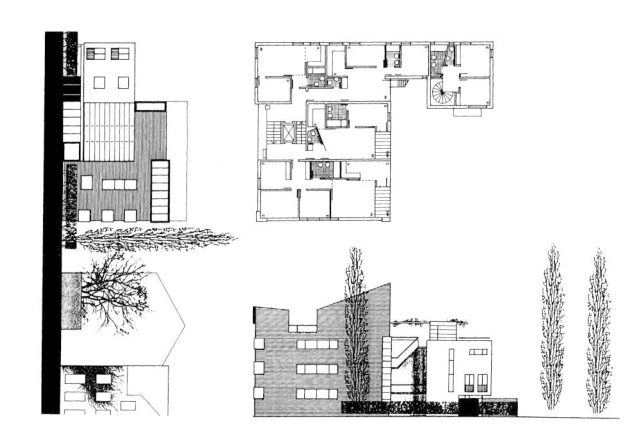

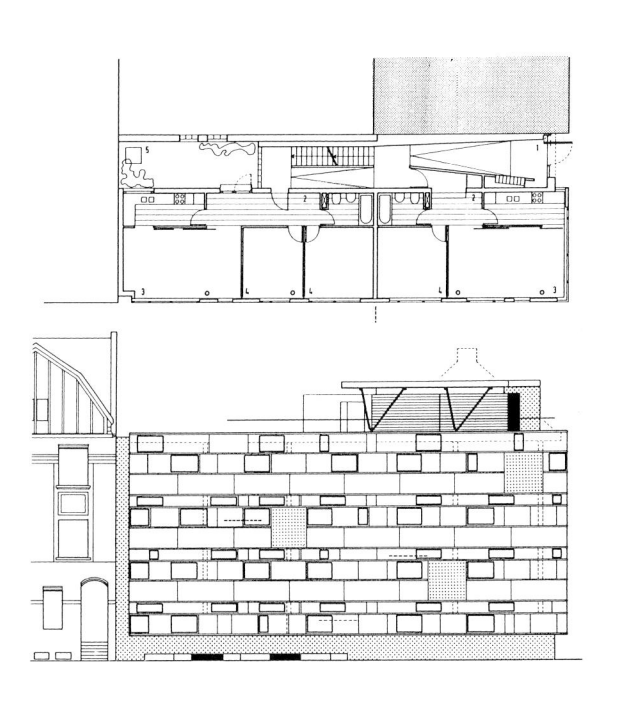

Drei Wohnprojekte:
1. Eckwohngebäude mit Glasfassade –
Duisburg 1996 (Wettbewerb, 2. Preis)
2. Kunstsammler-Villa mit Holzfassade –
Münster 1996
3. Bohlweg Apartment Haus – Münster 1996
(Wettbewerb, 1. Preis)

Three Residential Projects:
1. Corner housing with glass façade –
Duisburg 1996 (Competition 2nd prize)
2. Art collector's villa with wooden
façade – Münster 1996
3. Bohlweg apartment building –
Münster 1996
(Competition 1st prize)

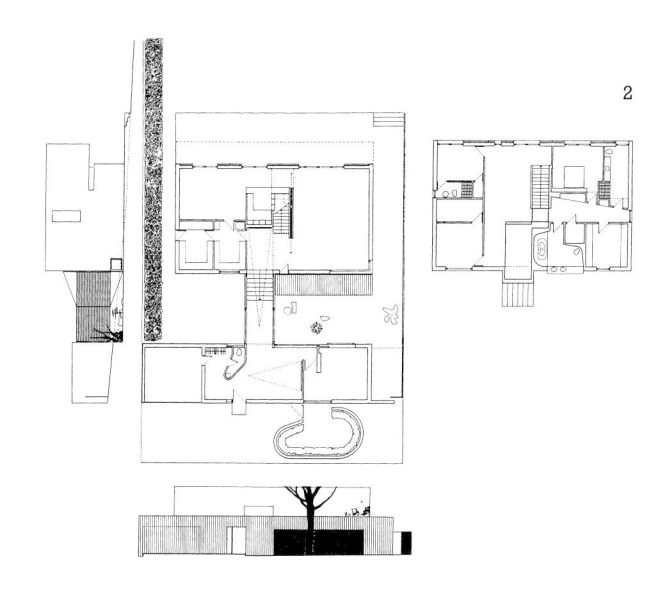

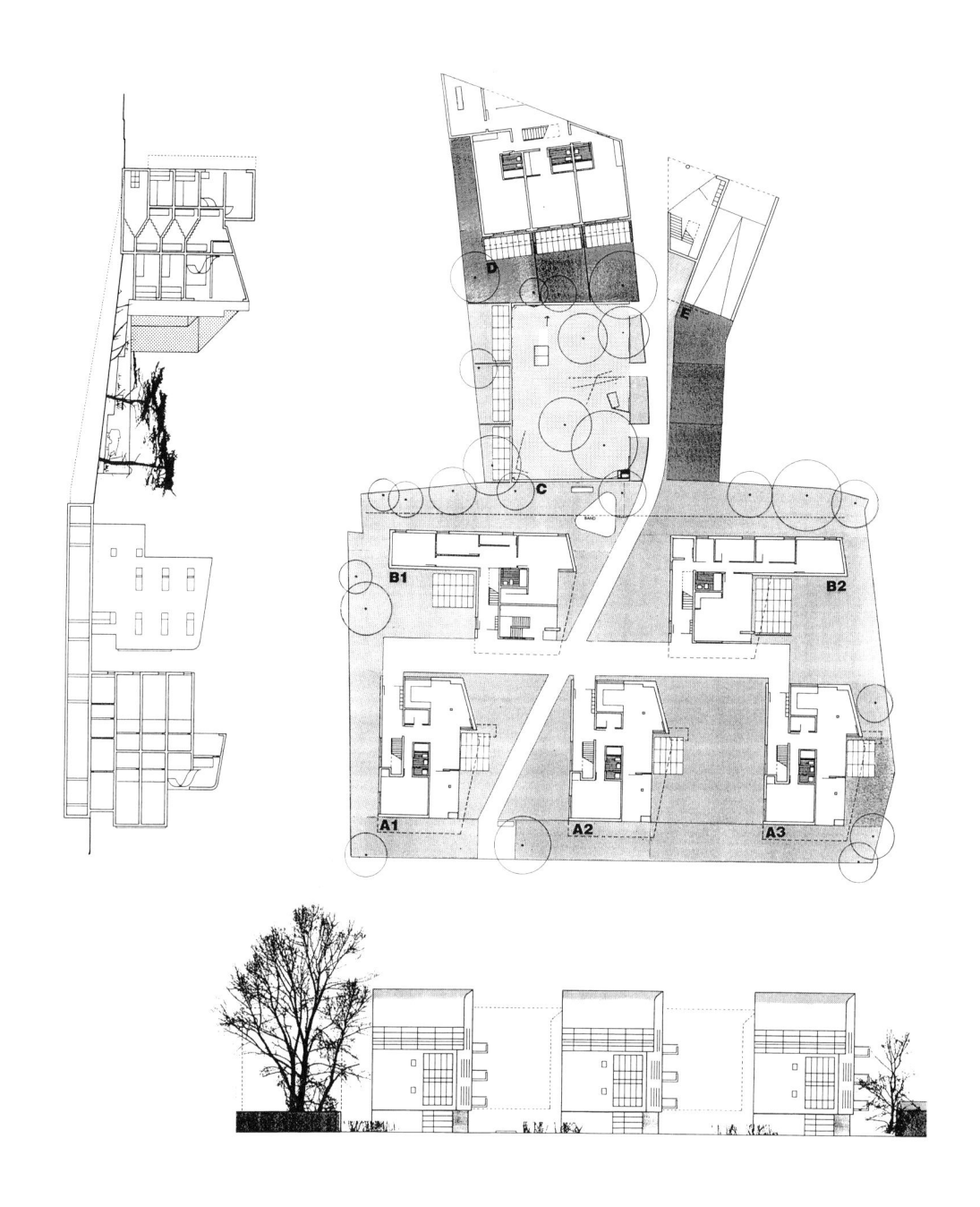

Matrix Villen – Castrop-Rauxel 1996–99
Zwei zur Straßenseite und fünf zur
Innenseite liegende Apartment-Blocks
(Wettbewerb, 1. Preis 1996).

    Matrix Villas – Castrop-Rauxel 1996–99
Two streetfront and five block
internal apartment buildings
(competition 1st prize 1996).

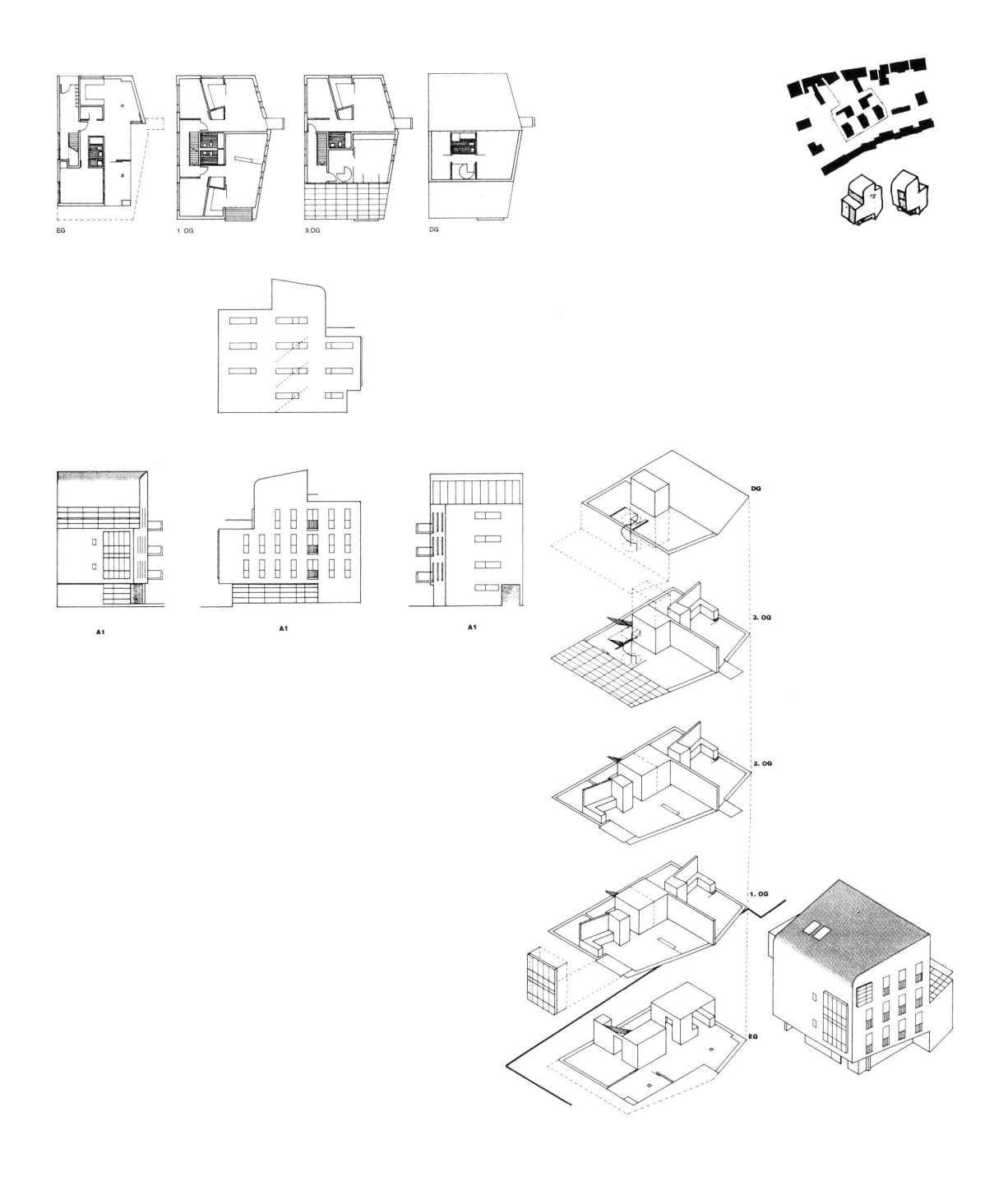

55 RESIDENTIAL PROJECTS

25 Apartments /
25 Apartments:
Bauherr/Client:
LVM Versicherungen
Standort/Location:
Bernhardstraße,
Münster
Fertigstellung/
Completion: 1997
Projektassistentin/
Project Assistant:
Karola Päch +
Elisabeth Böckenhoff-
Diekmann
Statiker/
Structural Engineer:
Motel & Schlicht
Techniker/Technician:
Ing.-Büro Feldmeier

In einen dichten, aber eher durchschnittlichen Kontext verwoben – ein einfacher Riegel – schwerer Sockel, verputzte Obergeschosse – eine überbrückte Straße. Die Nord-Süd-Ausrichtung erlaubt Terrassen sowohl für straßen- als auch gartenorientierte Apartments.

Woven into a tight but unexceptional context – a simple slab – solid base, plastered upper floors – a street bridged. The north-south alignment allows terraces for both street and garden oriented apartments.

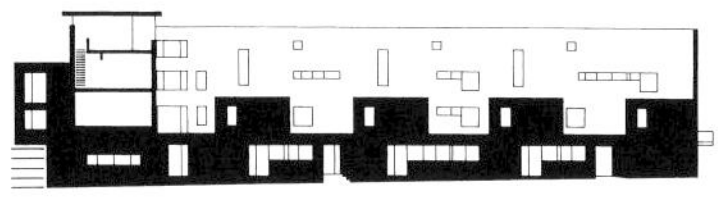
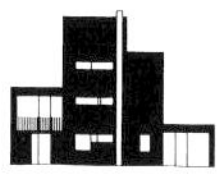
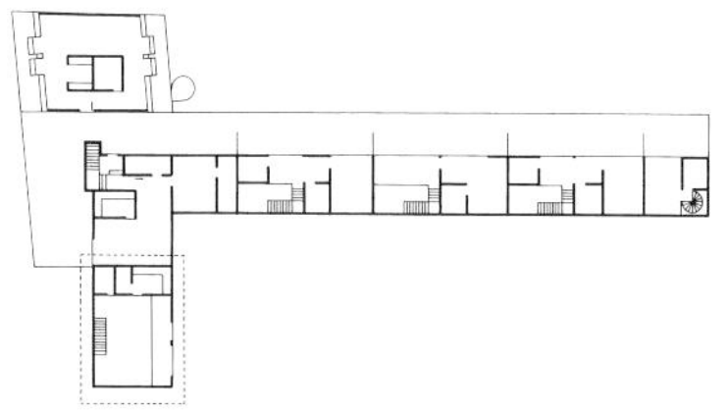
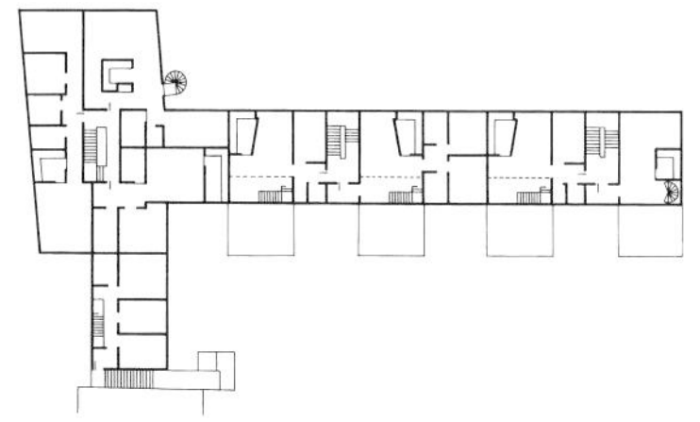
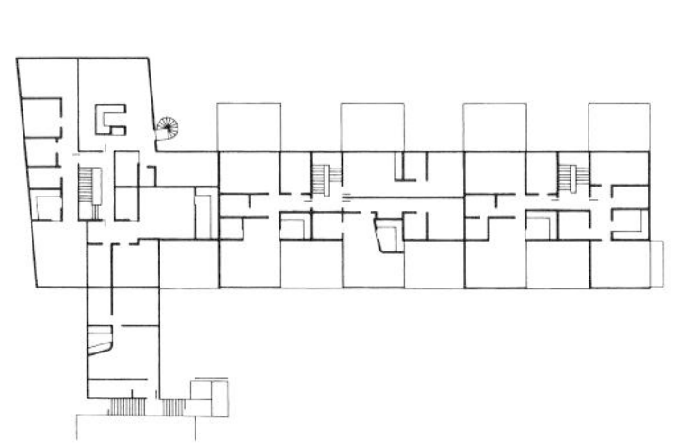
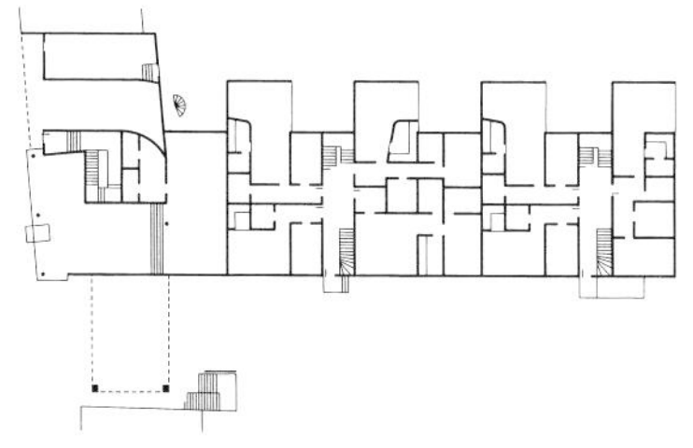
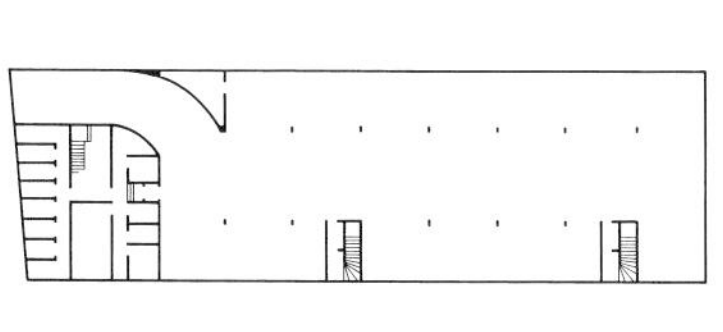
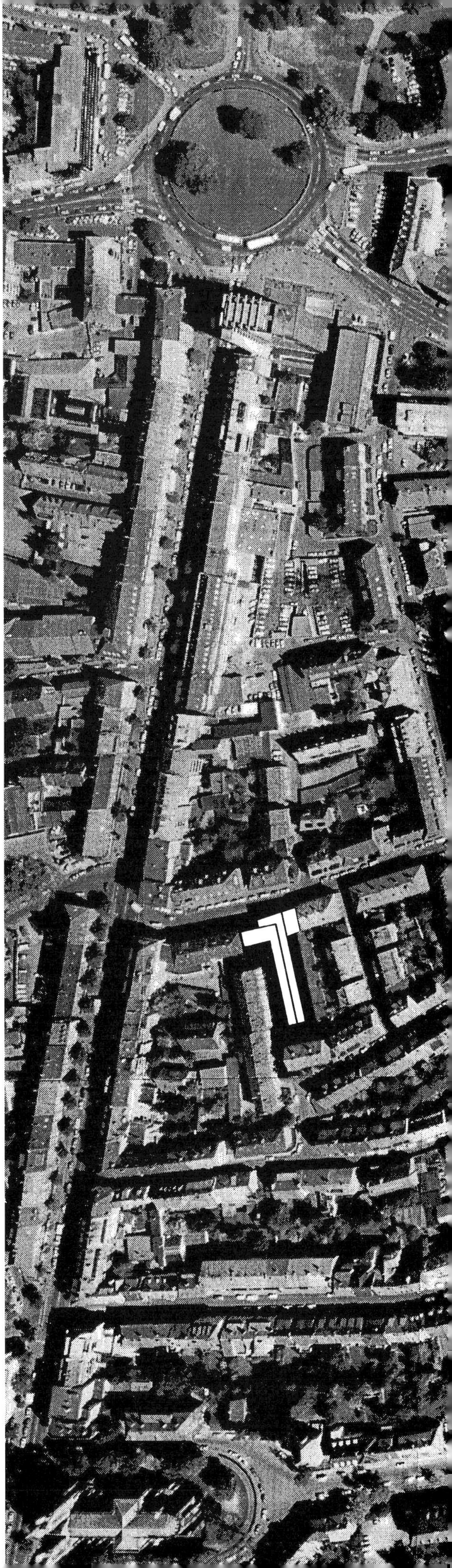

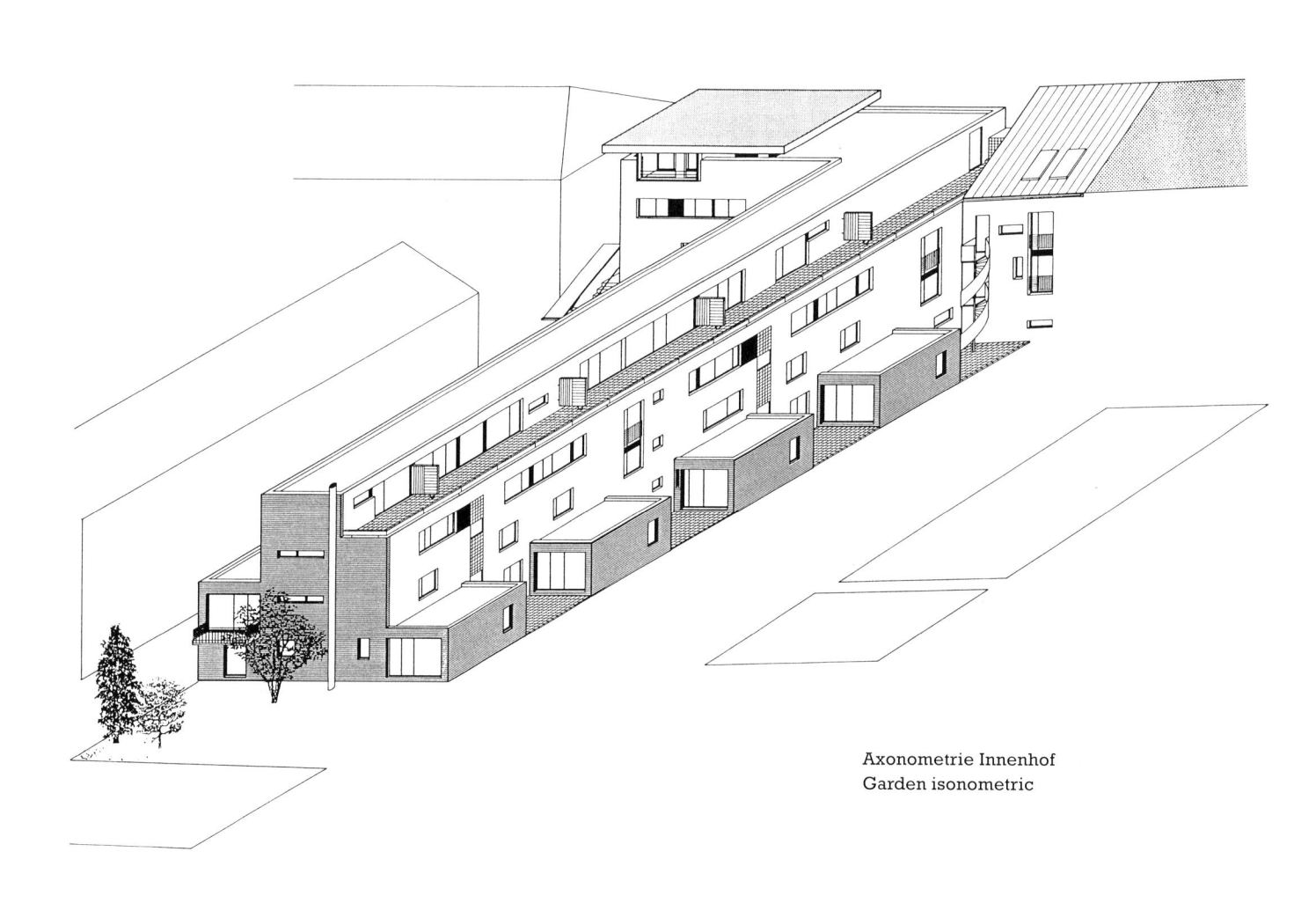

Axonometrie Innenhof
Garden isonometric

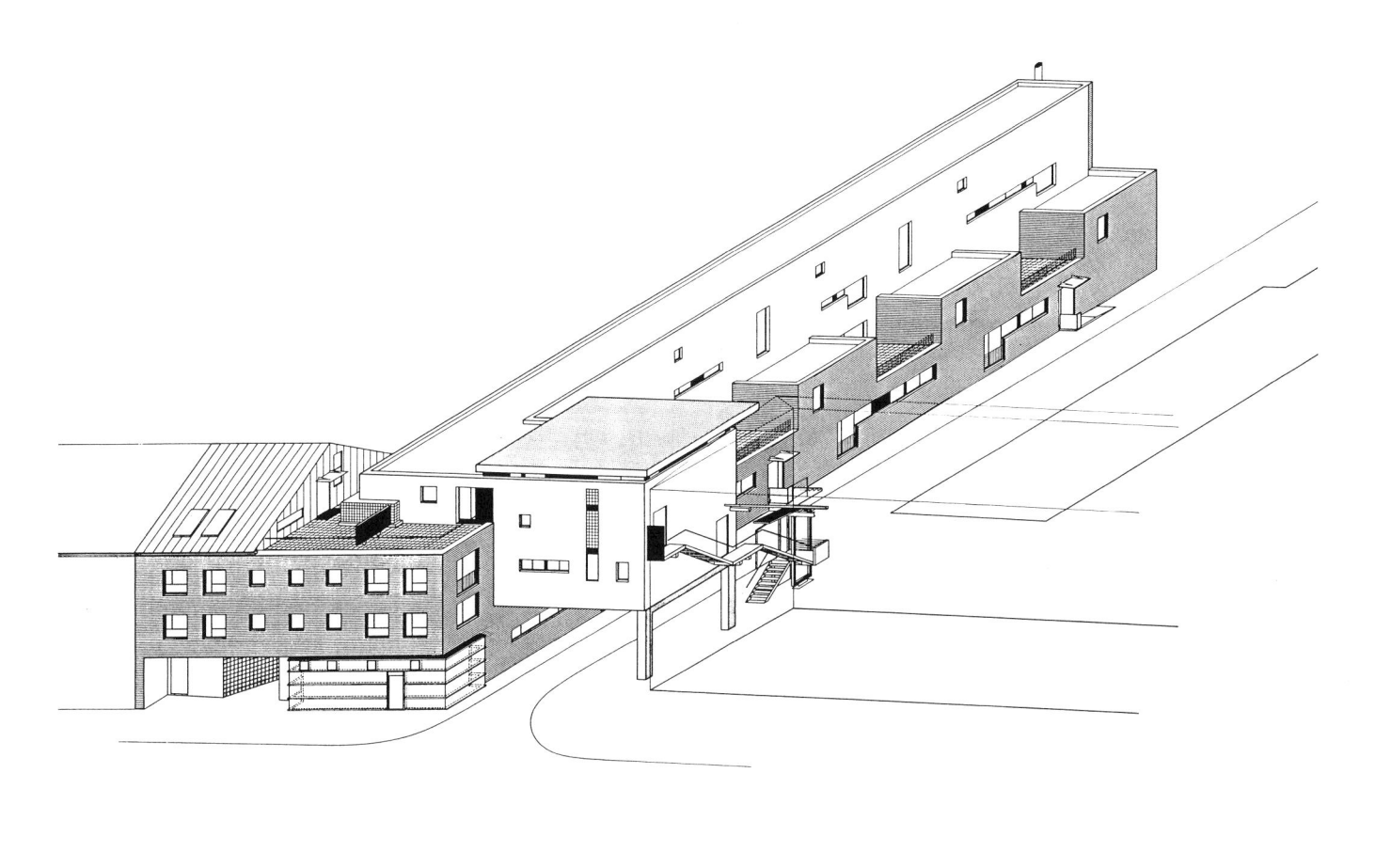

Axonometrie Straße
Street isonometric

Baustelle / Site

59 RESIDENTIAL PROJECTS

Eurolandschaft
Euro-Landscape

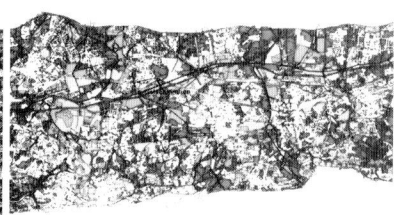

Barcelona-Block city   Rhein/Ruhr-Fragmented city

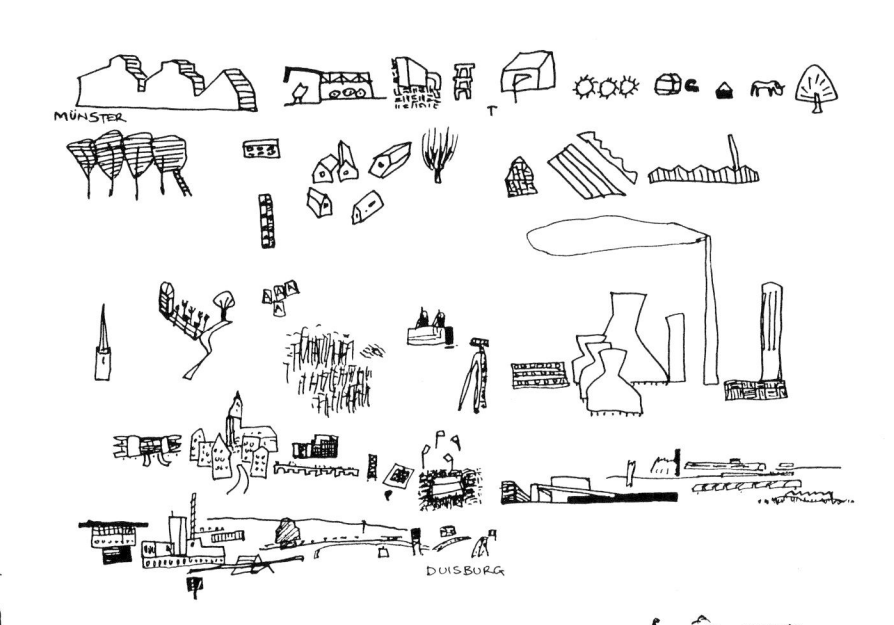

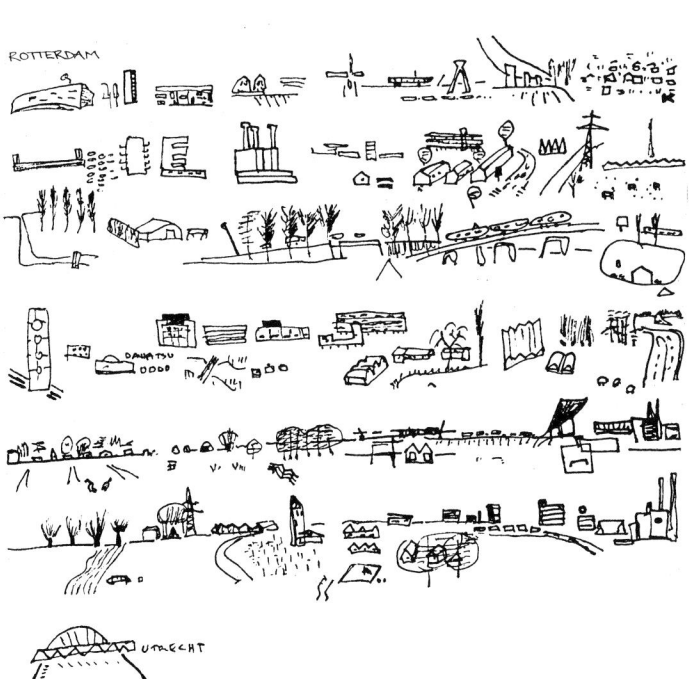

Eurolandschaft Schnitte/Euro-Landscape sections

Heute, gegen Ende des 20. Jahrhunderts, kann das Siedlungsmuster Europas am besten nachts von einem Flugzeug aus verstanden werden. Zu erkennen ist ein beinahe flächendeckendes Netz von Transportwegen, von verstreuten Industrie-, Wohn- und Freizeitbereichen. Die historische Stadt ist hier nur einer von vielen Knotenpunkten. Ein »Innerhalb« und »Außerhalb« gibt es nicht mehr, lediglich örtliche Grenzen zwischen unterschiedlich beschaffenen Texturen. Die Natur – die einst die Ortschaften umgab – ist nun selbst umgeben. Heute benötigen die landwirtschaftlichen Flächen und Parks die Mauern, die früher zum Schutz der Städte dienten.

Die heute zunehmend verstreute städtische Landschaft ist ein Ergebnis der technologischen Entwicklung. Unsichtbare Informationen, Medien und Kommunikationstechnologien machen die Notwendigkeit von physischer Nähe überflüssig. Die überall verbreiteten Infrastruktur- und Straßennetzwerke ermöglichen dem Personenverkehr und dem Containerverkehr einen einfachen Zugang zu fast allen Punkten auf der Landkarte. Dieses Modell ähnelt mehr und mehr einem gleichmäßig verbreiteten Teppich und immer weniger dem herkömmlichen Modell der monozentrischen Stadt.

Als klar gegliederte und geozentrische Einrichtung ist die Stadt vom gewöhnlichen Zustand bzw. dem »Außerhalb« zu unterscheiden, während sich der »Teppich« in einem ganz anderen Maßstab manifestiert. Man kann heute sagen, daß er mit variierender Dichte vom Mittelmeer bis zur Nordsee reicht. Mehr Zustand als Ort, allgegenwärtig, selbst mit sporadisch physischen und sichtbaren Manifestationen, ist er aufgrund aggressiver Transport- und Informationsnetze stets immanent.

Wie die fokussierte Stadt frühere soziale Hierarchien, die zentralisierte Regierung und Verteilungssysteme repräsentierte, so spiegelt heute der Teppich das Ausmaß der Verbreitung der Mediendemokratie wider – jedem Menschen sein Auto. Während unsere

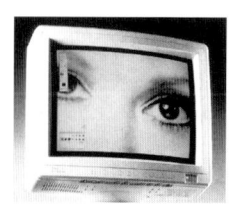

Now, at the end of the twentieth century, the habitation pattern of Europe is best understood from an aeroplane at night. What can be seen is an almost ubiquitous network of transport routes and scattered industrial, residential and leisure fields. The historic city here is just one of many nodes. There is no longer an inside and an outside, only local borders between differing textural conditions. Nature – that which once surrounded – is now itself surrounded. It is the agricultural zones and the parks, which today require the walls that once protected cities. Today's increasingly dispersed urban landscape is a result of technological evolution. Invisible information, media and communications technologies do away with the need for physical proximity. Ubiquitous infrastructure networks and freeway grids allow easy individual or containerised access to almost any point on the map. This model resembles more and more a carpet of equal distribution and less and less the inherited model of the monocentric city.

A focussed and geocentric event, the city is distinguishable from the general condition, or »outside«; the carpet manifests at an entirely different scale. It can now be said to extend with varying density factors from the Mediterranean to the North Sea. More condition than place, ubiquitous even with sporadic physical and visible manifestations, it is always, through aggressive transport and information nets, immanent.

As the focussed city represented past social hierarchies, centralised government and systems of distribution, so the carpet today reflects the extent of media-democracy – every-man in his car. While our hearts may remain in the historic city, it seems that we are destined to increasingly traverse the fields of business parks, rampant housing sub-divisions, explosions of »hypermarkets«, airports, exit ramps and leisure parks.

Visual coherence is absent in this new city. This does not mean that it is random. It belongs to a higher

STADTBÜCHEREI BW 1993 - INNENSTADT

MÜNSTER

YELLOW WARENHAUS BW 1993

63   EURO-LANDSCAPE

Herzen noch an der historischen Stadt hängen, scheinen wir dazu bestimmt, die Bereiche der Gewerbegebiete, des zügellosen Häuschenbauens, der sich explosionsartig vermehrenden Hypermärkte, Flughäfen, Autobahnzufahrten und Freizeitparks immer öfters durchqueren zu müssen.

Eine visuelle Kohärenz ist in dieser neuen Stadt nicht vorhanden – was nicht heißen soll, daß sie willkürlich ist. Sie ist Teil einer höheren Komplexitäts-Ordnung und muß unter den Rahmenbedingungen der Mobilität verstanden werden. Die Zeit hat physische Distanz ersetzt als das, was zusammenfügt oder trennt. Diese neue, lose und instabile Geographie umgeht die Planungen der traditionellen, städtischen Administration.

Infrastrukturelle Schnittpunkte, Korridore, offene Räume und Zugangspunkte (Bahnhöfe und Flughäfen) müssen nicht länger als Barrieren, sondern als lokalisierte Knotenpunkte gesehen werden, wo Interessenskonflikte den Anstoß zu gestalteten Interventionen liefern, zur Entwicklung neuer, spekulativer städtischer Szenarien.

Augen, die nicht sehen – Augen, die hindurchsehen.

In den zwanziger Jahren schrieb Le Corbusier: »...niemand kann heutzutage die Ästhetik leugnen, die sich von den Werken der modernen Industrie loslöst.« Durch Ersetzen von »moderner Industrie« durch »Informationstechnologie« können die Umstände unserer derzeitigen Situation sofort bestimmt werden. Die Konsequenz der neuen virtuellen Realität, der Computernetze und der allgegenwärtigen Sprache des Fernsehens ist eine entgegenwärtigende, verflüchtigende und entschwindende Transparenz, die alle Dinge und Orte infiziert hat.

Diese neue Freiheit, die Freiheit des losgelösten Betrachters, ermöglicht das, was Le Corbusier »eine gewagte Umstellung« genannt hat. Wenn wir uns »frischen Blickes« umschauen, finden wir uns in einer neuen Art von Landschaft wieder. Während unsere Modelle von virtueller und tatsächlicher Landschaft sich zu überschneiden beginnen, beginnen wir, in unserer alltäglichen Umgebung »eine Schönheit zu entdecken, die ruhig, vital und stark ist«.

Die »Eurolandschaft« verkörpert dieses neue Feld. Die Lektionen des Monitors infiltrieren nicht nur unseren Wahrnehmungsapparat, sondern strukturieren auch unsere greifbare Welt. Dieser kontinuierliche Teppich ist das Feld, der Strom zeitgenössischer Erfahrung und Ereignisse.

Es ergibt sich eine Matrix, die nicht mehr mit kartesischer Geometrie gemessen oder geordnet werden kann. Ein leichterer Zugang kann gefunden werden,

order of complexity and must be understood within the framework of mobility. Time has substituted physical distance as that which joins or separates. This new loose and unstable geography side-steps planning and traditional urban administration.

Infrastructural intersections, corridors, open spaces and entrance points are no longer to be seen as barriers, but as localised nodes where conflicting overlaps of interest provide the incentive for designed intervention, the development of new speculative urban scenarios.

Eyes which do not see – eyes which see through.

In the 1920's, Le Corbusier wrote »...nobody today can deny the aesthetic which is disengaging itself from the creations of modern industry«. Substituting »Information Technology« for »Modern Industry« locates instantly the conditions of our present situation. The consequence of the new virtual reality, networked computers, and the ubiquitous language of television are a de-presencing, an ephemeralising, a seeping transparence which has infected all things and all places.

This new freedom, the freedom of the dislocated viewer, makes possible what Le Corbusier went on to call »a daring transposition«. If we look around »with a fresh eye« we find ourselves in a new landscape. As our models of virtual and actual landscape begin to overlap, we also see in our everyday surroundings »a beauty that is calm, vital and strong«.

The Eurolandschaft is this new field, the lessons of the monitor not only infiltrating our perceptual apparatus, but also structuring the tangible world. This continuous carpet is the field, the flux of contemporary experience and of contemporary events.

It is a matrix that can no longer be measured or ordered by Cartesian geometry. It can be accessed better using the language of computer modes and menus (cut-out – format – help – copy – pattern – transfer – shift – index, etc.).

Today's »accusing lines«, event horizons, and field patterns demand a reinvention of mapping techniques, syntax and terminology.

ELSEWHERE – beyond the perceptual horizons of an event. EVENT – as connection looses its significance, the principle element in the new thematic template becomes the autonomous incident (Event Type – Event Frequency). DEGREE OF EMPTINESS – negative intensity between events. SCALE – size itself no longer impresses, time has replaced distance as the everyday measure. TOPOGRAPHY – Corridors and nodes of movement (railways, freeways, and airports) are communal spaces today. ARCHITECTURE – as a

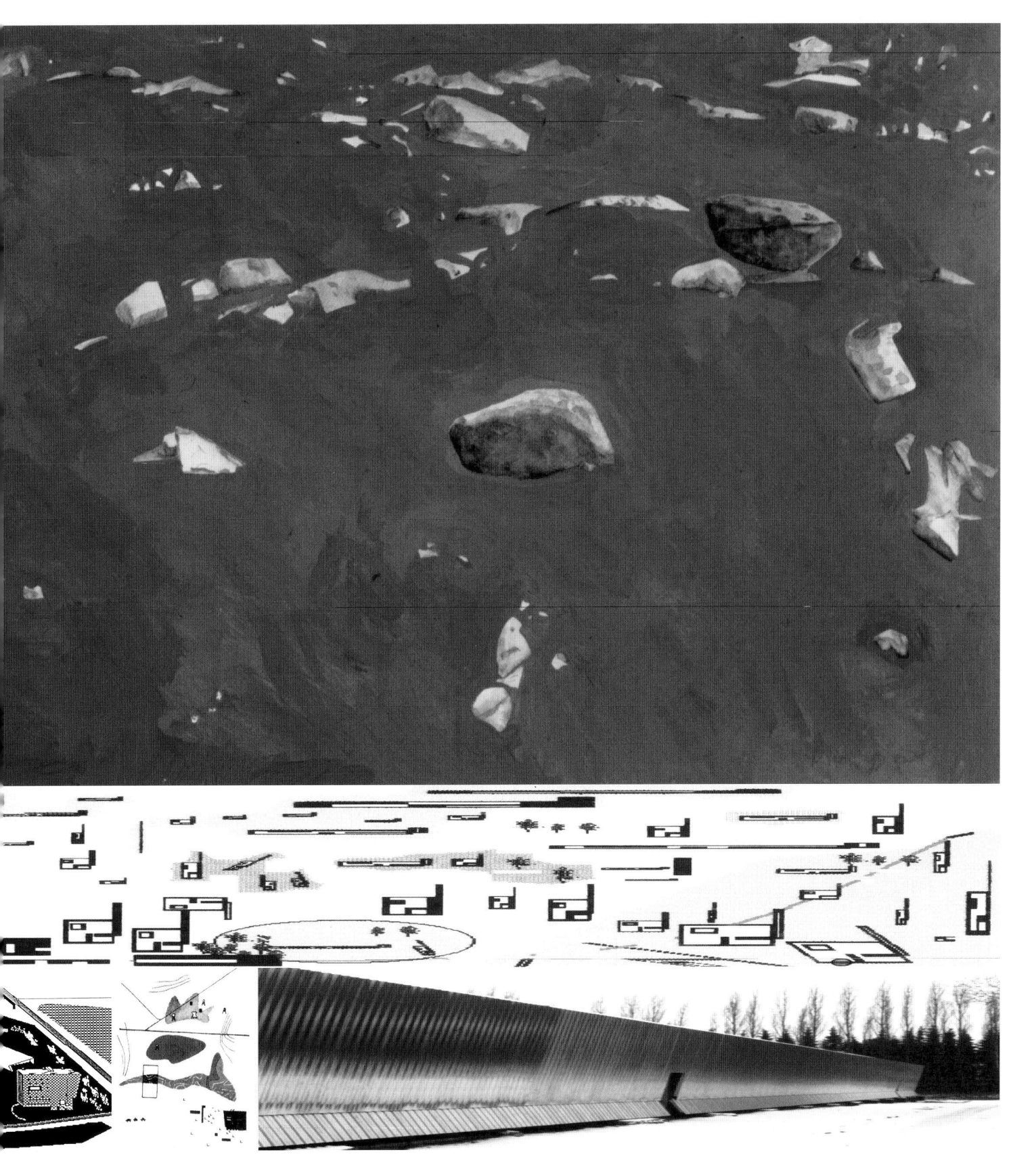

Steine – Gewerbehallen / Rocks – sheds

65 EURO-LANDSCAPE

wenn man die Sprache der Computermodi und -menüs gebraucht (cut-out – format – help – copy – pattern – transfer – shift – index, etc.).

Die heutigen »anklagenden Linien«, Ereignishorizonte und Feldmuster erfordern die Neuerfindung der Vermessungstechnik, Syntax und Terminologie.

ANDERSWO – jenseits der wahrnehmbaren Horizonte eines Ereignisses. EREIGNIS – da die Verbindung an Bedeutung verliert, wird das wichtigste Element in der neuen Themenschablone zum autonomen

relatively infrequent event in the Euro-Landscape, the self-conscious object has the option to hold fast, to solidify, to sediment, to become a fixed island against which surrounding tidal shifts can be measured – mass in the age of media.

Ereignis (Ereignistyp – Ereignishäufigkeit). GRAD DER LEERE – negative Intensität zwischen Ereignissen. MASSSTAB – Größe allein beeindruckt nicht mehr, die Zeit hat die Distanz als alltägliche Maßeinheit ersetzt. TOPOGRAPHIE – Korridore und Bewegungsknotenpunkte (Schienen, Autobahnen, Flughäfen) sind heute kommunale Räume. ARCHITEKTUR – als relativ seltenes Ereignis in der Eurolandschaft hat das selbstbewußte Objekt die Option, festzuhalten, zu verdichten, zu gründen, eine feste Insel zu bilden, an der die sie umgebenden »Gezeitenwechsel« gemessen werden können – Masse im Medienzeitalter.

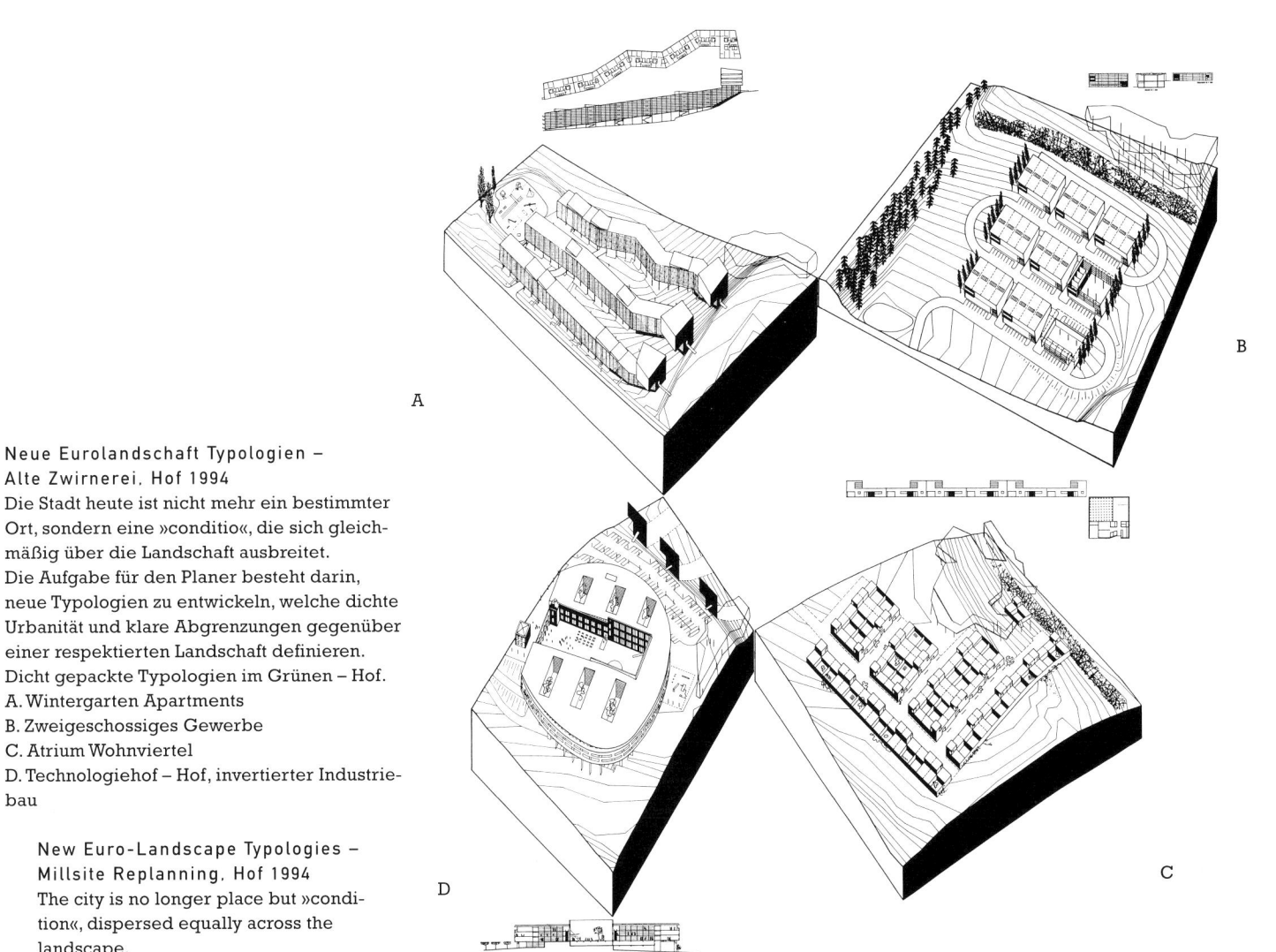

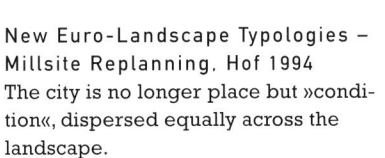

Neue Eurolandschaft Typologien –
Alte Zwirnerei, Hof 1994
Die Stadt heute ist nicht mehr ein bestimmter Ort, sondern eine »conditio«, die sich gleichmäßig über die Landschaft ausbreitet.
Die Aufgabe für den Planer besteht darin, neue Typologien zu entwickeln, welche dichte Urbanität und klare Abgrenzungen gegenüber einer respektierten Landschaft definieren.
Dicht gepackte Typologien im Grünen – Hof.
A. Wintergarten Apartments
B. Zweigeschossiges Gewerbe
C. Atrium Wohnviertel
D. Technologiehof – Hof, invertierter Industriebau

New Euro-Landscape Typologies –
Millsite Replanning, Hof 1994
The city is no longer place but »condition«, dispersed equally across the landscape.
The challenge for planning is to develop new typologies that juxtapose density with respected landscape.
Close packed typologies in green – Hof.
A. Wintergarden apartments
B. Stacked sheds
C. Atrium precinct
D. Technology centre – Hof, inverted factory

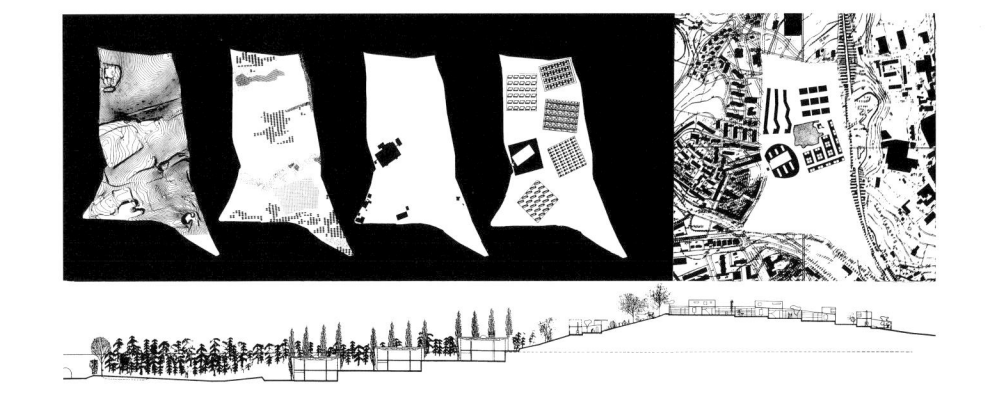

Medizinisches Dienstleistungszentrum
Medical Service Centre

Bauherr/Client:
B+P Projektregie GmbH
Standort/Location:
Erin-Gelände, Castrop-Rauxel
Fertigstellung/Completion: 1996
Projektassistent/Project Assistant:
Jürgen Zils
Statiker/Structural Engineer:
Ing.-Büro Burmann
Techniker/Technician:
Ing.-Büro Werder

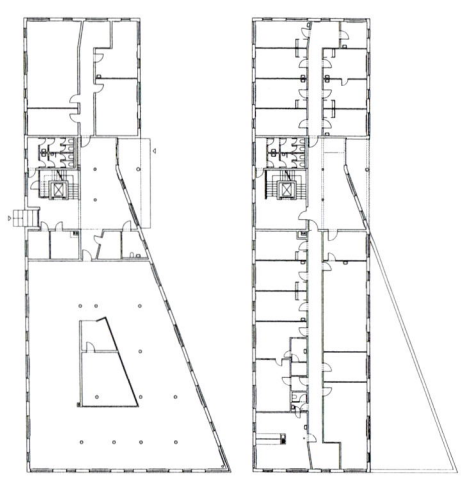

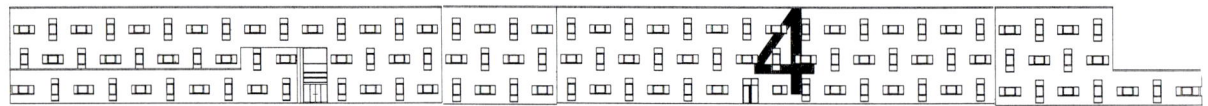

Grundrisse und durchlaufende Fassade / Plans and continuous façade

Ein typisches »Eurolandschaft Ereignis« – eine für ein minimales Budget von Investoren gebaute Kiste. Derlei drakonische Kostenlimits schließen formalen oder materiellen Ausdruck aus – Fassadenartikulation ist daher auf die Rotation des Standardfensters begrenzt. Ergebnis: die endlos verwobene Fassade – eine Versöhnung vielleicht von Perrets bevorzugtem, vertikalen (Himmel – Erde) Fenster und Le Corbusiers Streifen (Horizont) Alternative.

A typical »Euro-Landscape Event« – a minimum budget, investor built box. Such draconian cost limits preclude formal or material expression – façade articulation is therefore limited to the rotation of the standard window. Result: the endless woven façade – a reconciliation perhaps of Perret's preferred vertical (sky – earth) window and Le Corbusier's strip (horizon) alternative.

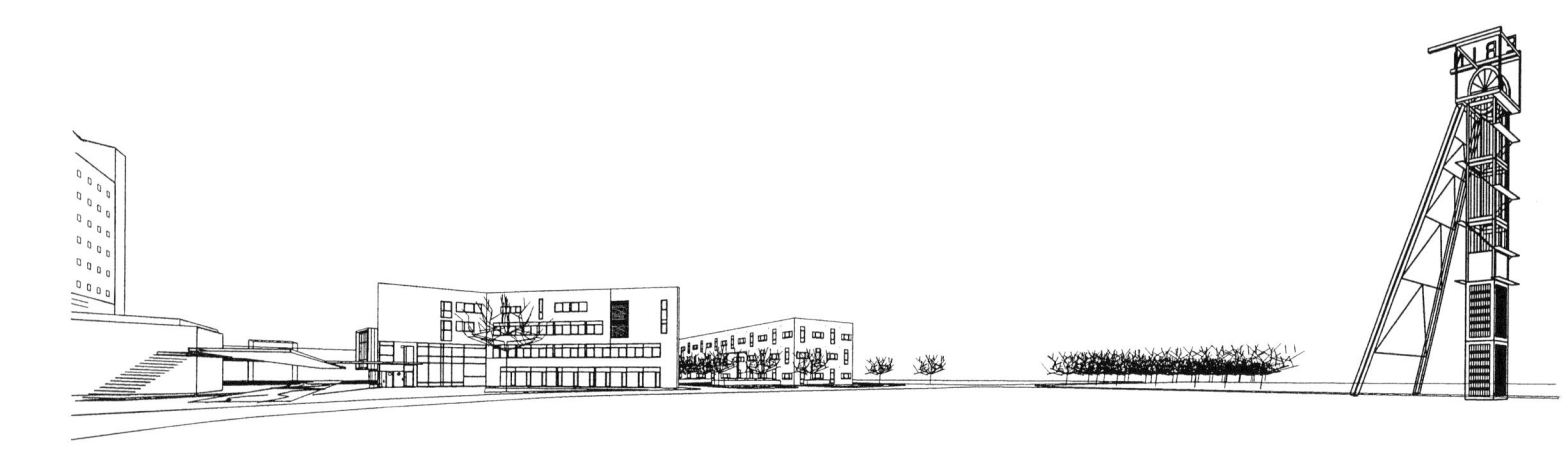

Gewerbepark Erin – Castrop-Rauxel
Eine Objektlandschaft (das heutige Äquivalent der jetzigen redundanten Industrielandschaft). Nur der »Pit Head« bleibt in der Stadt, in der Nähe der Leere der restrukturalisierten Zeche Erin. Knappschaftsgebäude und DIEZE sind zwei der ersten kolonisierenden Objekte in diesem postindustriellen Eurolandschaftsfeld.

Business Park Erin – Castrop-Rauxel
A landscape of objects (today's equivalent of the now redundant landscape of industry). Only the »Pit Head« remains in the city near emptiness of the reconstituted coal mine. The Knappschaft and DIEZE are two of the first colonising objects in this post industrial Euro-Landscape field.

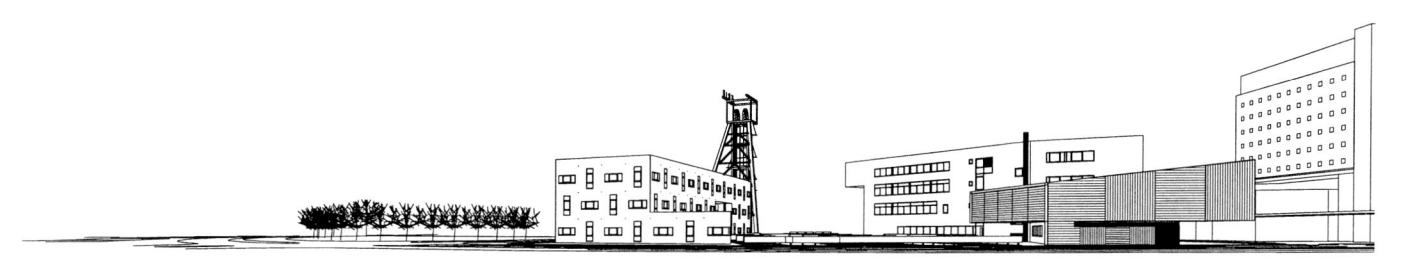

Gewerbegebiet = Objekt-Landschaft / Business Park = landscape of objects

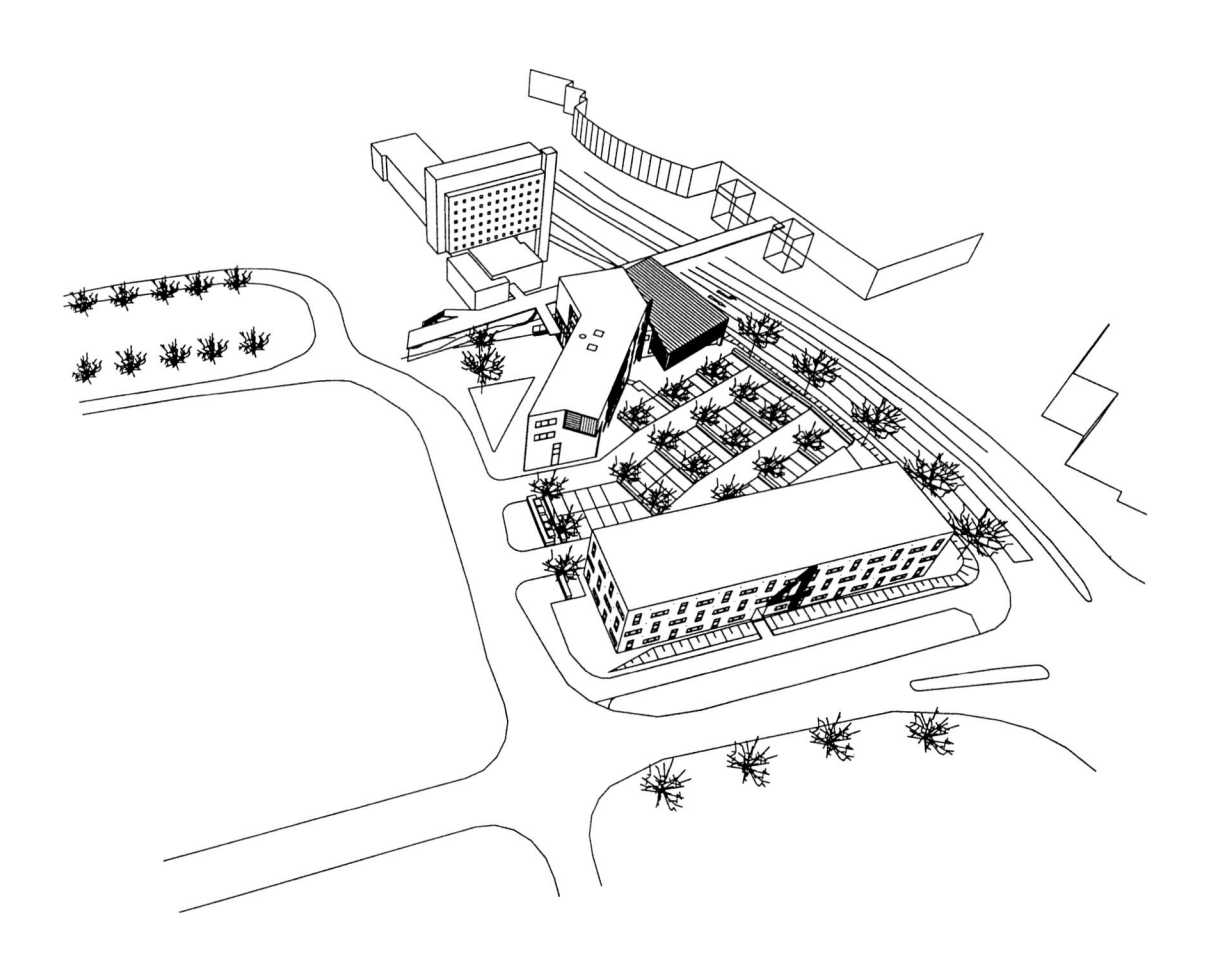

71 MEDICAL SERVICE CENTRE

Dienstleistungszentrum
Business Service Centre

Bauherr/Client:
GeWo, Gemeinnützige Wohnungsgesellschaft
Standort/Location: Landschaftspark Erin (ehem. Zechengelände), Castrop-Rauxel
Fertigstellung/Completion: 1996
Projektassistent/Project Assistant: Andreas Kimmel, Jürgen Zils
Statiker/Structural Engineer: Motel & Schlicht
Techniker/Technician: Werning & Dr. Schmickler

DIEZE Weiter- und Umbildungszentrum
Ein Zweig der Fernuniversität Hagen und das Zentrum »Frau in Beruf und Technik« teilen sich Konferenz- und Seminareinrichtungen.

DIEZE Educational Building
A branch of the Open-University Hagen and a Women's Retraining Center – shared conference and seminar facilities.

Ankerbox mit geometrischen Erweiterungen.
Das ungewöhnliche Konferenzelement kragt
akrobatisch aus.

Anchor box plus geometric extensions.
The alien conference element cantilevers
acrobatically.

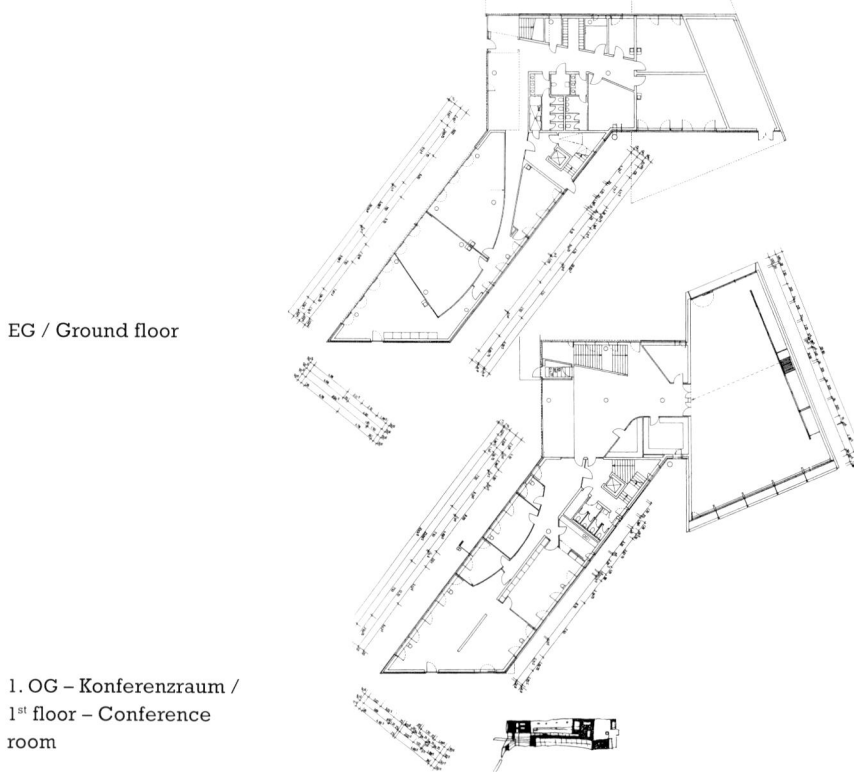

EG / Ground floor

1. OG – Konferenzraum /
1ˢᵗ floor – Conference
room

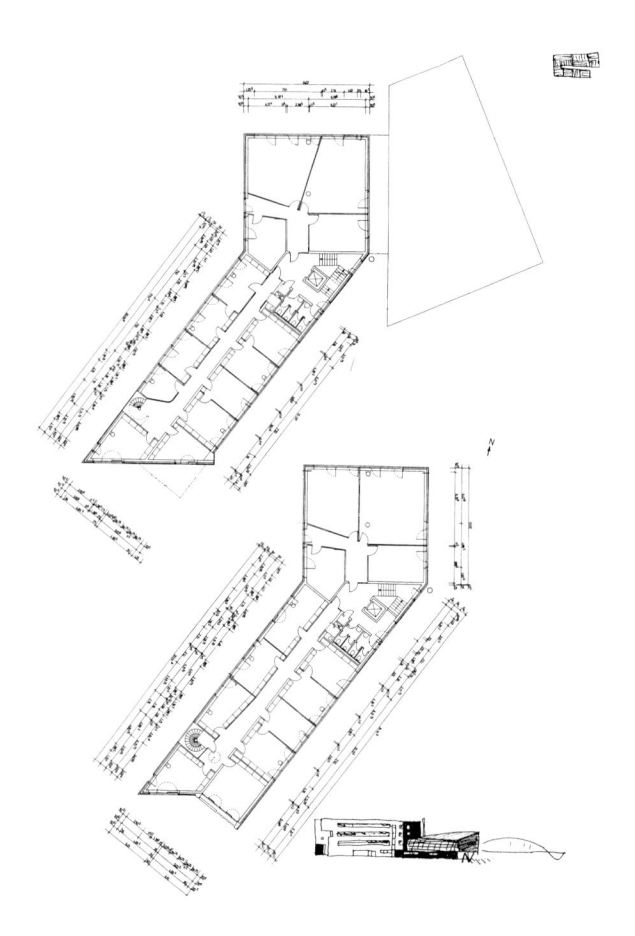

2. OG – Seminarräume
und Büros / 2ⁿᵈ floor –
Seminar rooms and
offices

3. OG – Seminarräume
und Büros / 3ʳᵈ floor –
Seminar rooms and
offices

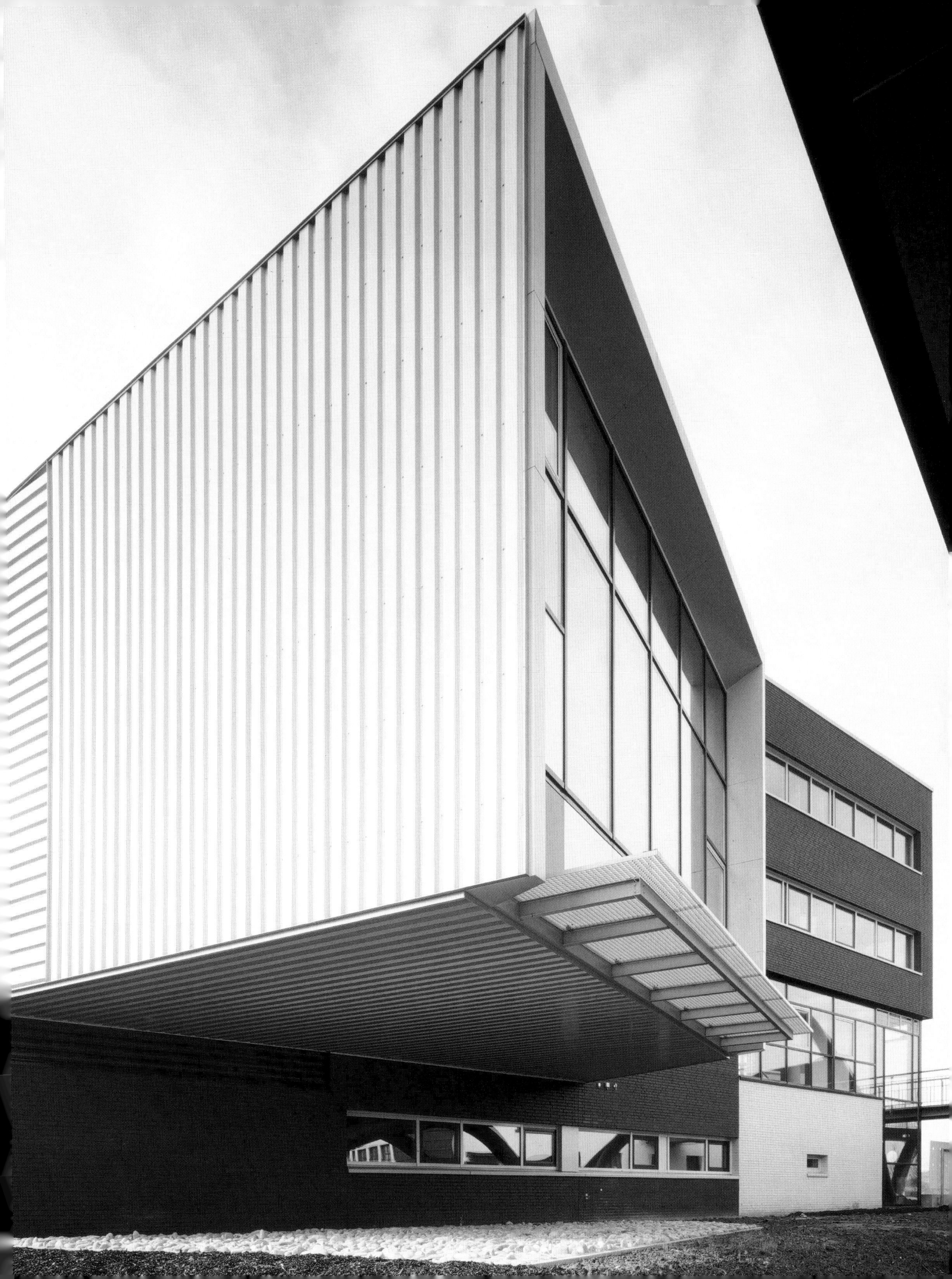

Boden- und Brückeneingänge /
Ground and bridge entrances

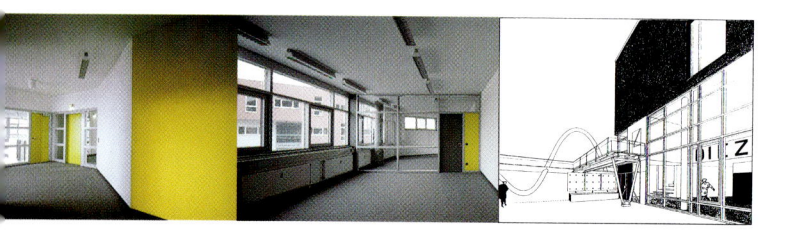

DIEZE – Eingangshalle
Strikte Plangeometrien entwickeln sich zu
einer äquivalenten, dreidimensionalen
Sprache von gefaltetem Material und Ebenen.

DIEZE – Entrance Hall
Strict plan geometries evolve into an
equivalent three-dimensional language of
folded material and planes.

Eingangshalle / Entrance hall

Konferenzhalle / Conference hall

Der Raum im 1. OG ragt TV-gleich hervor, sich der Brücke nähernd.
The 1st floor room cantilevers TV-like to the bridge.

Norden = hoch–eng / North = high–narrow
Süden = niedrig–weit / South = low–wide

78 DIENSTLEISTUNGSZENTRUM

Treppe – Detail / Stair – detail

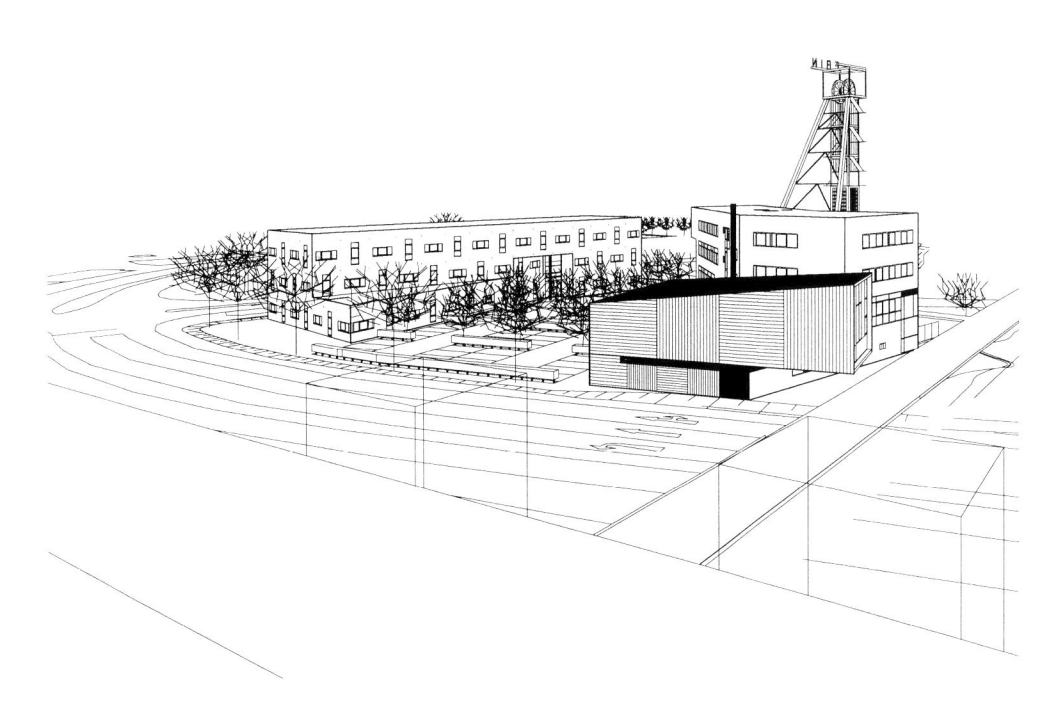

79 BUSINESS SERVICE CENTRE

Eurolandschaftsblick / Eurolandscape view

DIEZE mit Konferenzsaalanhänger / DIEZE with conference box adjacency

Albeda Schule
Albeda College

Bauherr/Client:
Albeda Schule /
Albeda College
Standort/Location:
Rosestraat,
Kop van Zuid,
Rotterdam
Fertigstellung/
Completion: 1996
Architekten/Architects: Kruisher Elffers
mit / with
Bolles+Wilson

Kopf / Head

Ostansicht / East elevation

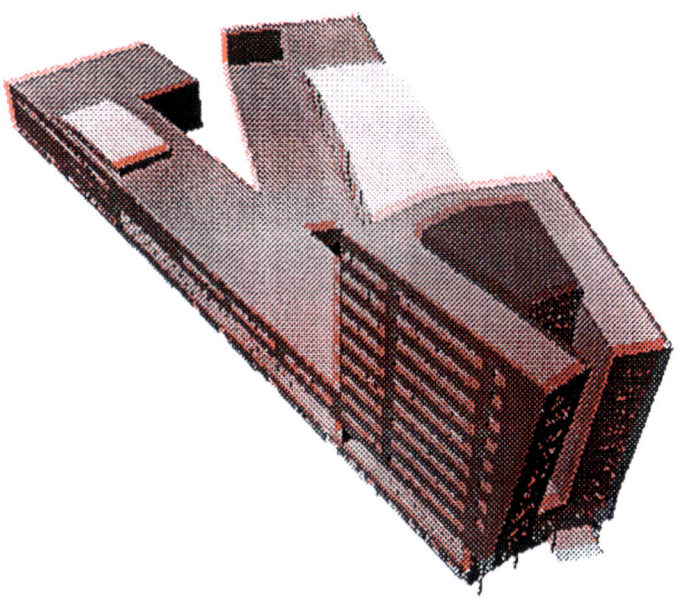

Formsprache als Kontextergänzung
Form language derived from context geometry

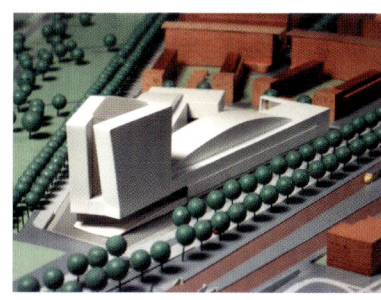

Kontext / Context

Entwurf / Design sketch

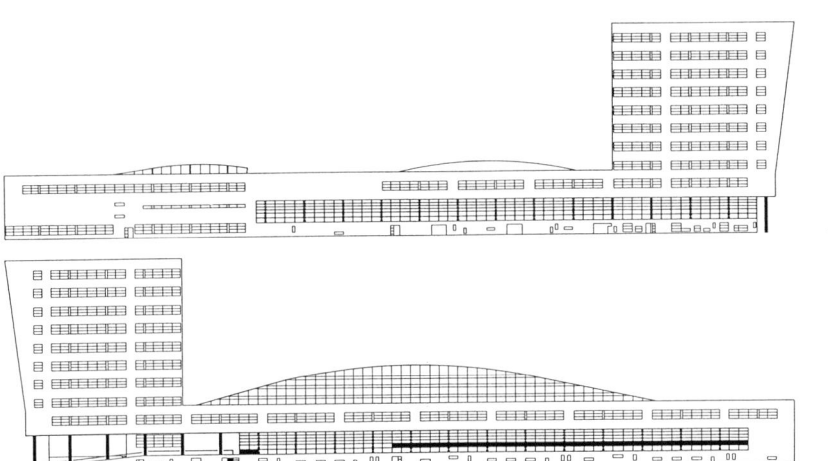

Masse ist hier das Thema – Masse erzeugt durch das spitz zulaufende Gelände. Ein geometrischer Endpunkt für das neue Kop van Zuid Wohngebiet. Die beiden niedrigen Arme beherbergen die Albeda Schule (Berufsausbildung), der Turm enthält die Prinzessin Margriet Schule (ärztliche Versorgung). Formale Klarheit ist hier nicht nur ein Resultat der wirtschaftlichen Einschränkung, sondern auch ein Resultat der Notwendigkeit, einem so großen Programm (25.000 m²) eine innere Hierarchie und dem umgebenden urbanen Feld eine externe Ordnung und Verankerung zu geben.

> Mass is here the subject – a mass generated by the tapering site – a geometric end to the new Kop van Zuid housing quarter. Low arms house the Albeda College (vocational training), the tower the Princes Margriet School (medical services). Formal clarity is here not only a result of economic restraints, but also of the need to give an internal hierarchy to such a large program (25,000 m²) and an external ordering and anchoring of the surrounding urban field.

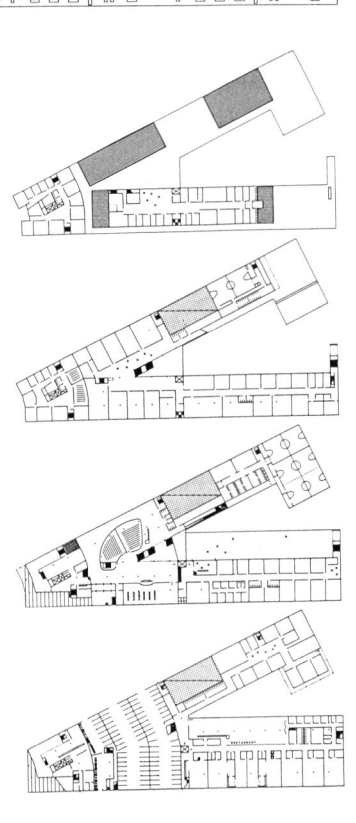

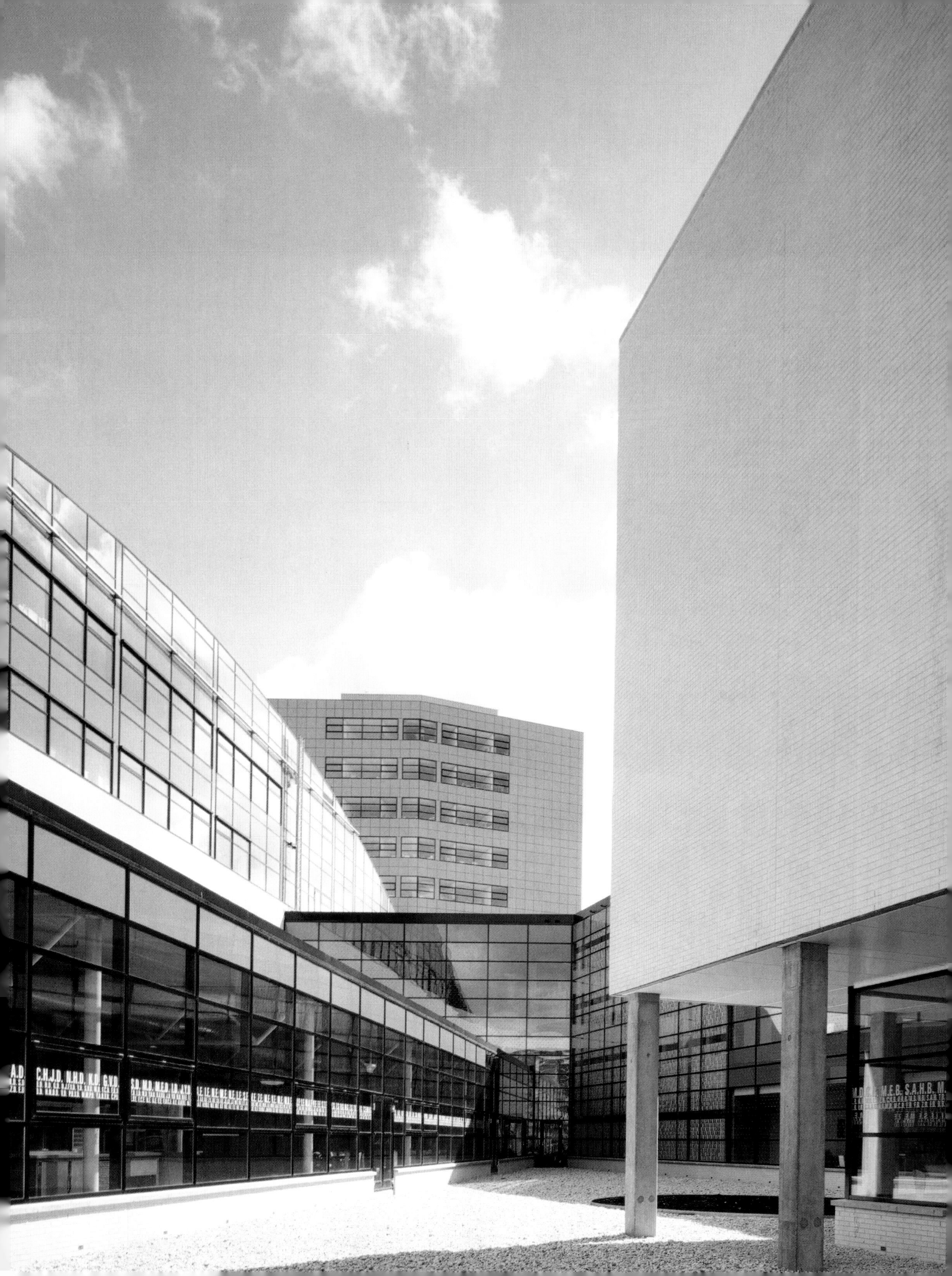

Hotel New York, Kai-Landschaftsgestaltung
Hotel New York, Quay Landscaping

Bauherr/Client:
Stadtplanungsamt
Rotterdam / City
planning office
Rotterdam
Standort/Location:
Wilhelminapier,
Kop van Zuid,
Rotterdam
Fertigstellung/
Completion: 1998

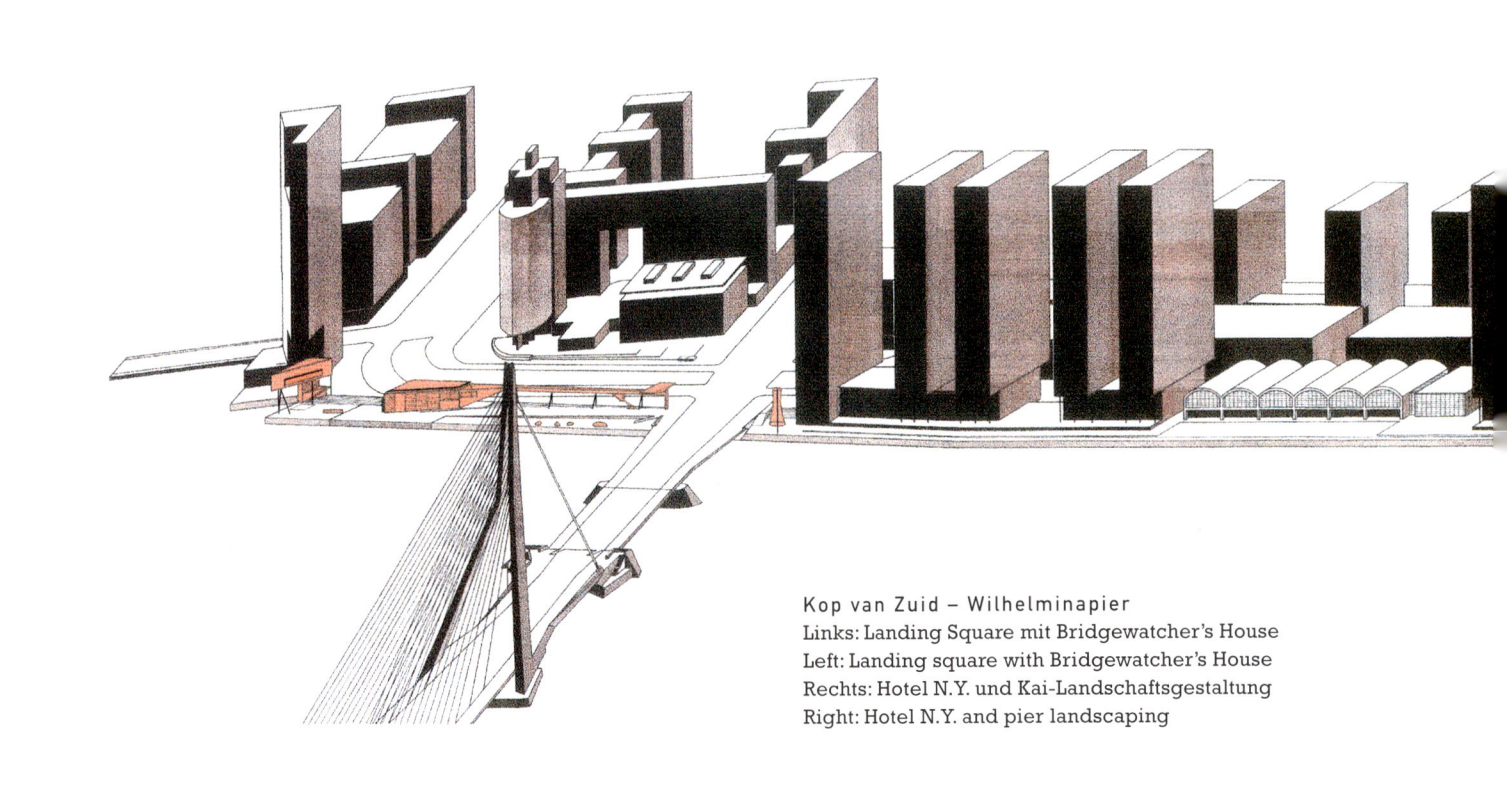

Kop van Zuid – Wilhelminapier
Links: Landing Square mit Bridgewatcher's House
Left: Landing square with Bridgewatcher's House
Rechts: Hotel N.Y. und Kai-Landschaftsgestaltung
Right: Hotel N.Y. and pier landscaping

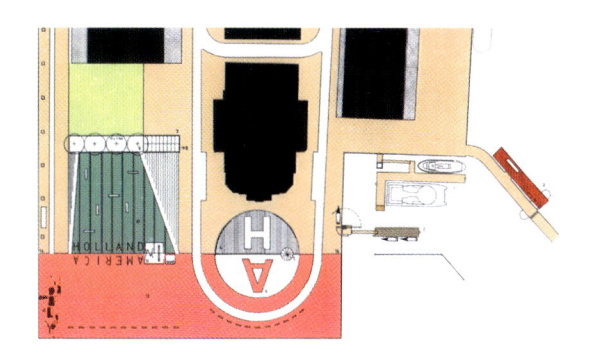

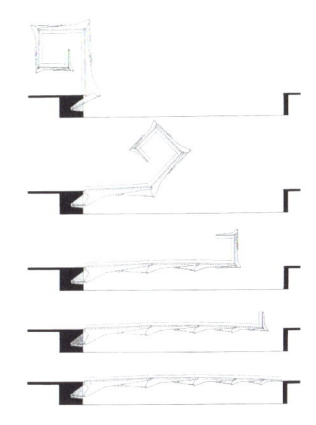

»Scorpion«-Hydraulik-
brücke / »Scorpion«
Hydraulic Bridge

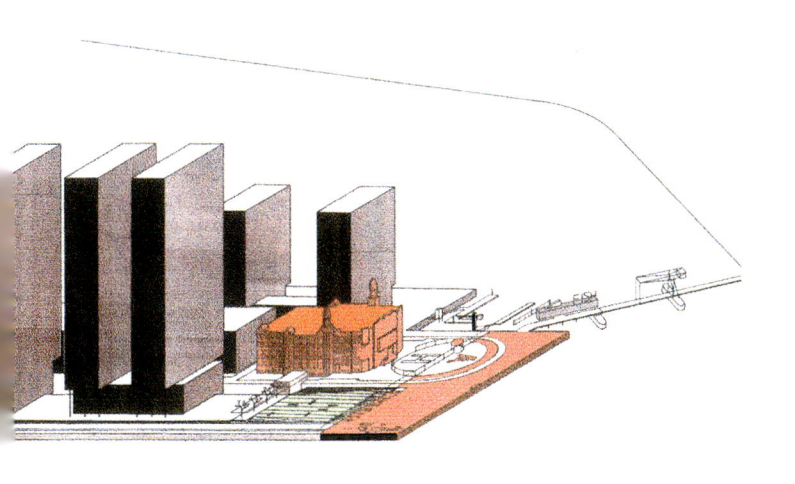

Wilhelminapier, Hotel New York, Koninginnenhoofd – Kai Landschaftsgestaltung
Das Wilhelminapier, Einschiffungsort für Emigration in die Neue Welt. Eine Verbindung und ein Distanzieren, das in der ikonographischen goldenen »Holland-Amerika«-Schrift auf der Fassade verkörpert ist. Die erste Frage war, welche Form das Ende des Wilhelminapiers haben sollte. Die Antwort war überraschend einfach – eine gerade Linie. Ein mythologischer Horizont, über dem, wie in einer Steinberg-Stadt, die Freiheitsstatue praktisch sichtbar ist. Bei der landschaftlichen Gestaltung des Piers ist dieser Horizont, diese Holland-Amerika-Grenze, ein bißchen in die holländische Richtung gerutscht. Das Ende des Piers ist designierter amerikanischer Raum – unbestimmter Raum, ein Ereignisfeld. Eine große Reihe von Aktivitäten sind hier möglich, sogar Kafkas großer Oklahoma Zirkus.
Auf der holländischen Seite der simulierten Grenze ist ein künstlicher Grashügel und das »Boardwalk« Hotel-Café. Autos können nach Amerika und zurück kreuzen. Ein Spielplatz überbrückt die Grenze (internationale Schaukel) und ein riesiges H und A aus rostfreiem Stahl beschreibt das Thema auf dem Boden.

Wilhelminapier, Hotel New York, Queens Head Quay –
Quay Landscaping
The Wilhelminapier embarkation point for emigration to the New World. A connection and a distancing embodied in the iconographic gold »Holland-America« written across the façade. The first question, what shape should the end of the Wilhelminapier have. The answer, surprisingly simple – a straight line. A mythological horizon over which, as in a Steinberg City, the Statue of Liberty is practically visible. In landscaping the Pier, this horizon, this Holland-America border, is slipped a little in the Dutch direction. The end of the Pier designated as »American space« – indeterminate space, an events field. All activities are here possible, even Kafka's grand Oklahoma Circus.
On the Dutch side of the simulated border is an artificial grass hill and the hotel »Boardwalk« cafe. Cars cruise in and out of America. A playground straddles the border (international swing) and a giant stainless steel H and A re-inscribe the subject on the pavement.

Kop van Zuid, Kai-Landschaftsgestaltung
Kop van Zuid, Quay Landscaping

Bauherr/Client: Stadt Rotterdam / City of Rotterdam
Standort/Location: Wilhelminapier Kop van Zuid, Rotterdam
Fertigstellung/ Completion: 1996
Projektassistent/ Project Assistant: Jim Yohe
Statiker und Kontaktbüro / Structural Engineer and Contact: ABT, Velp
Elektrotechniker/ Electricial Technician: ETIS

Wilhelminapier –
Kop van Zuid Rotterdam 1991–96
In Verbindung mit Rotterdams neuer Erasmus-Brücke (Ben van Berkel) und der Entwicklung dieser Dockland Zone, sind Bolles+Wilson seit 1991 damit beschäftigt, die Landschaft der Wasserfront und den Landungsplatz zu orchestrieren – zentraler Punkt des neuen Kop van Zuid Distrikts.

Die Sprache, die sich auf diesem ersten Kai entwickelte, wurde in nachfolgenden Projekten weiterentwickelt, um andere Limits dieses speziellen Teils der Stadt zu definieren – Landschaftsgestaltung Hotel New York, West-Horizont der Wilhelminapier Bürotürme – Albeda Schule, südlichster Zipfel der Kop van Zuid Wohnblöcke – Neues Luxor Theater, architektonischer und kultureller Höhepunkt am Landepunkt der neuen Brücke.

Der Kai – ein Deck, das auf Beinen in der Masse steht, hat die Aufgabe, den urbanen Maßstab vom Büroturm und Verkehrsfluß auf das des Individuellen zu reduzieren.

Die Kolonnade, ein schwebender Stahlbalken, trennt den Kai von der Straße, ohne die spektakuläre Aussicht auf die Skyline zu blockieren. Dieser Balken kann auch überquert werden, eine Brücke, eine Station, die den Betrachter in das Zentrum der Bühne des Hafenpanoramas versetzt.

Zwei weitere Objekte markieren die Limits des Kais. Im Osten ein Arbeitsgebäude, das Bridgewatcher's-House, Steuerstelle der Brücken, Choreograph der Schiffahrt. Im Westen der Turm der Elektronischen Zahlen – eine leuchtende Eruption von nützlichen und nutzlosen digitalen Informationen.

Wilhelminapier
Kop van Zuid Rotterdam 1991–96
In conjunction with Rotterdams new Erasmus Bridge (Ben van Berkel) and the development of this Docklands zone, Bolles+Wilson have since 1991 been involved in orchestrating the waterfront landscape and the Landing Square – centre stage of the new Kop van Zuid district.

The language developed on this first quay has extended in subsequent projects to define other limits of this particular piece of city – Hotel New York landscaping, west horizon of the Wilhelminapier office towers – Albeda College, southern tip of Kop van Zuid housing blocks – New Luxor, centre architectural and cultural focus at the landing of the new bridge.

The Quay – a deck standing on legs in the mass – has the task of reducing the urban scale from office tower and traffic flows to that of the individual.

The Colonnade, a hovering steel beam, divides quay from street without blocking spectacular skyline views. This beam is itself traversable, a bridge, a station suspending the viewer centre stage in a harbour/city panorama.

Two further objects mark the limits of the quay. To the east, a working building, the Bridgewatcher's House, opener of bridges, choreographer of shipping. To the west, the Tower of Electronic Numbers – a glowing eruption of useful and useless digital information.

Kai Landschaftsgestaltung
Kop van Zuid Rotterdam 1991–96
Der Kai befindet sich vor den Hochhaustürmen des neuen Geschäftsdistriktes. Was hier gefragt ist, ist, den Maßstab von dem des großen, urbanen Ereignisses zu dem des individuellen herunterzubringen, Wasserfront als öffentlicher Raum.
OBERFLÄCHEN Eine gestreifte Rampe aus blauem Basalt verbindet Straße und Brückenebene zum unteren Kai, eine Fläche, die sich teppichähnlich über die Kante des Kais ins Wasser faltet. Zwei niedrigere, rauhe, granitgepflasterte Räume werden von der Rampe umrahmt, ein Garten der Fixierten Nummern und ein Feld der Elektronischen Steine.
OBJEKTE
1. Das Bridgewatcher's-House. Den Ausblick auf die Stadt dahinter einrahmend, kontrollierend – ein Gebäude, das von der Hafengesellschaft belegt ist. Von hier wird der Schiffsverkehr und die beweglichen Brücken auf der Maas orchestriert.
2. Stahl-Kolonnade und Restaurant. Der Platz dahinter ist durch einen transparenten Screen mit Eckdach und oberem Fußweg umschlossen.
3. Turm der Elektronischen Zahlen. Im Westen, am Anfang des Wilhelminapiers – ein Zeichen kommender Aktivität.

Quay landscaping
Kop van Zuid Rotterdam 1991–96
The Quay is located in front of the towers of the new business district. What is here required is to bring the scale down from that of the major urban event to that of the individual – waterfront as public space.
SURFACES Connecting street and bridge level to the lower quay is a striped ramp in blue basalt, a plain that folds carpetlike over the edge of the quay and into the water itself. Two lower rough granite paved spaces are framed by the ramp, a Garden of Fixed Numbers and a field of Electronic Rocks.
OBJECTS
1. The Bridgewatcher's House. Framing views of the city beyond, controlling – a building occupied by the Harbour Company. From here shipping traffic and the lifting bridges on the Maas are orchestrated.
2. Steel Colonnade and Restaurant. The Square behind is enclosed by a transparent screen with corner roof and upper walkway.
3. Electronic Tower of Numbers. To the west, at the start of the Wilhelminapier – a sign of the coming activity.

Kai-Zeichnung und Planungsstudie für Platz/Kai-Integration. »Roter Klecks« – (zukünftiges Luxor Theater) als autonomes Gradelement im urbanen Plan definiert.
Quay sketch and planning study for square/quay-integration. »Red Blob« – (Future Luxor Theatre) defined as autonomous hinge element in the urban plan.

KOP VAN ZUID

Brückenentstehung – Landentstehung –
Kolonnadenplan und Ansichten mit
zukünftigem Restaurant – Kai Layout
Rechts: Elektronische Steine

Bridge making – Land making –
colonnade plan and elevation with future
Restaurant – Quay layout
Right: Electronic Rocks

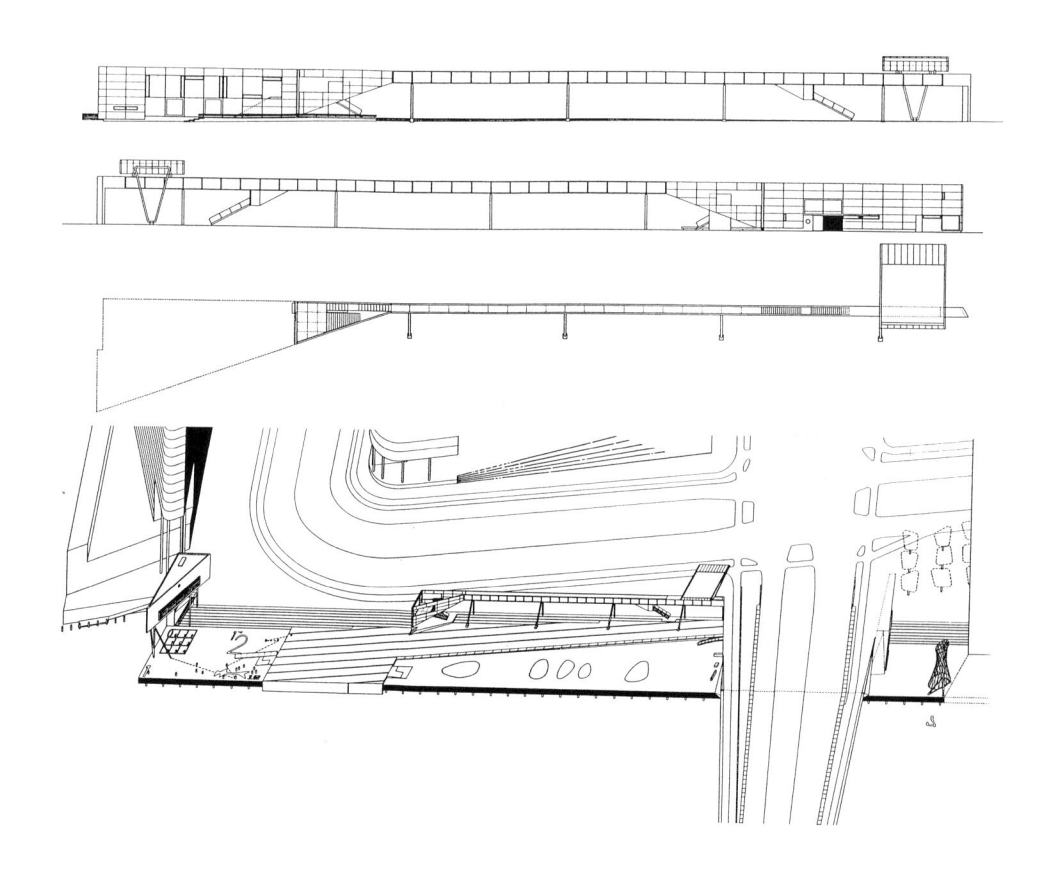

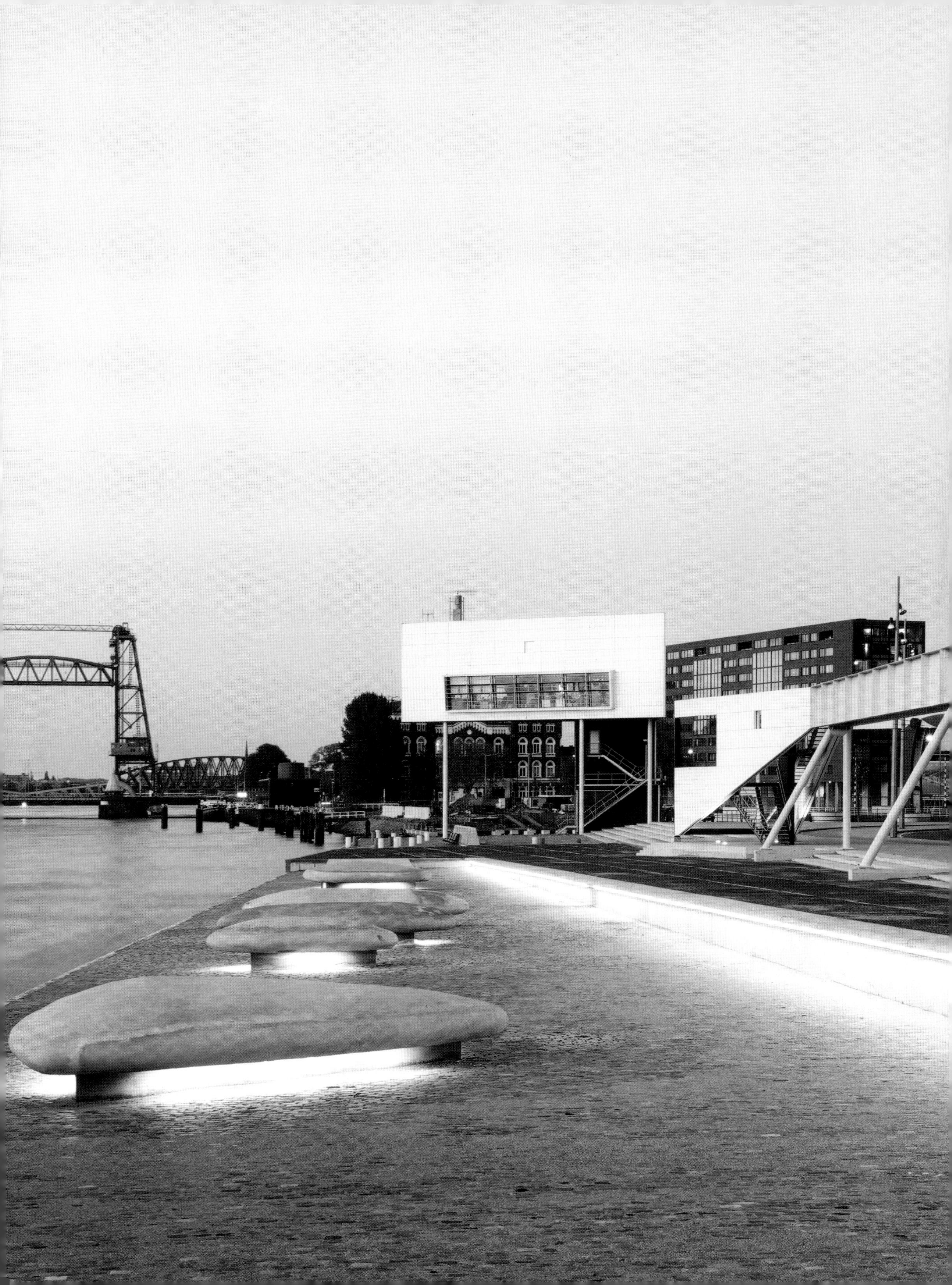

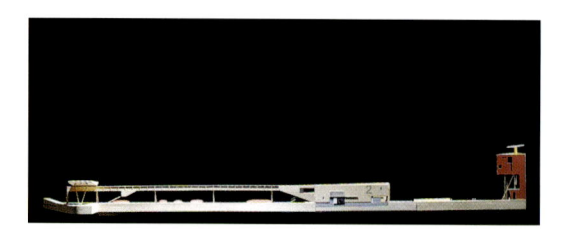

Südansicht Planungsmodell /
South elevation planning model

Kolonnade: ein überquerbarer Balken – 360° Ausblick / Colonnade: – A traversable beam – 360° view

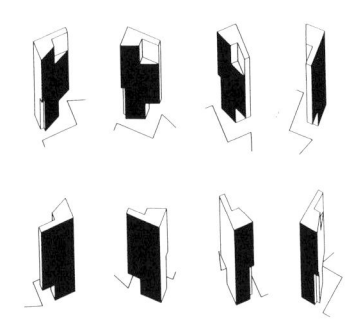

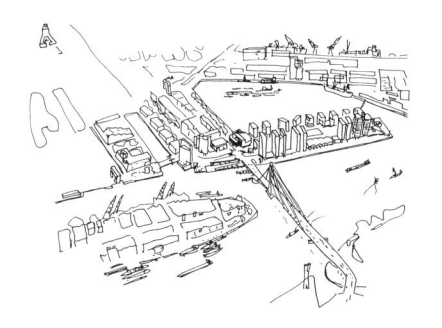

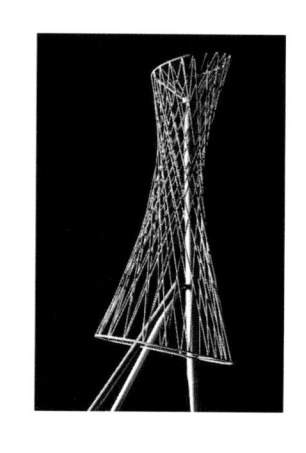

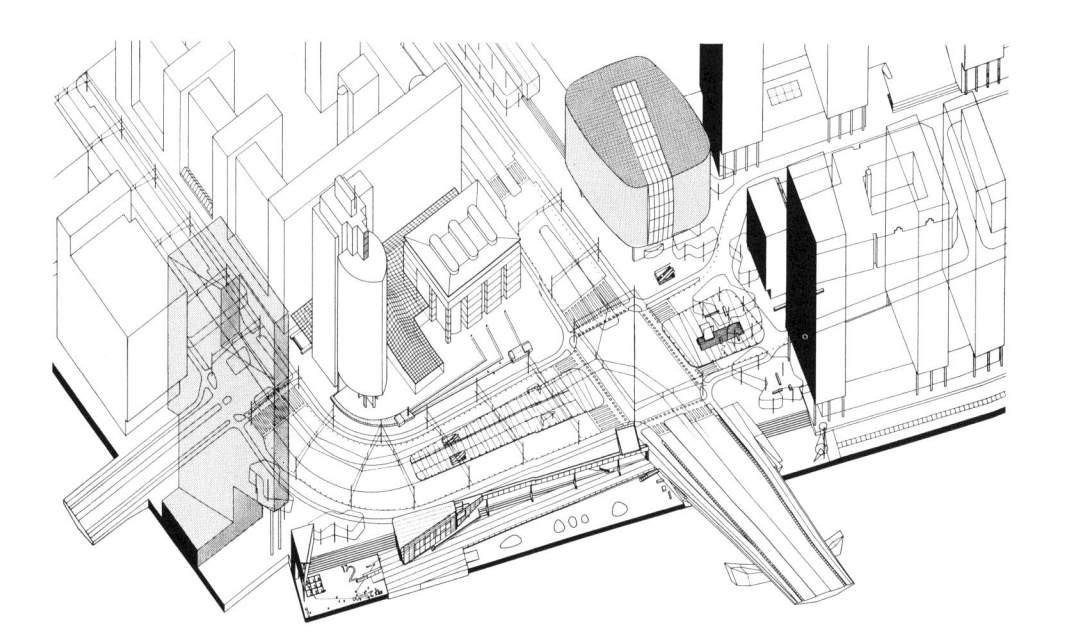

Urbane Hektik – Planungsstudie Verkehrs- und Straßenlayout – Turm der beweglichen Zahlen – Dynamisches Flußufer – Dynamischer Turm, Massenstudie

Urban hectic – Planning study traffic and street layout – Moving Number Tower – Dynamic riverbank – Dynamic tower, mass study

Rechts: Stille / Right: stillness

96 KOP VAN ZUID

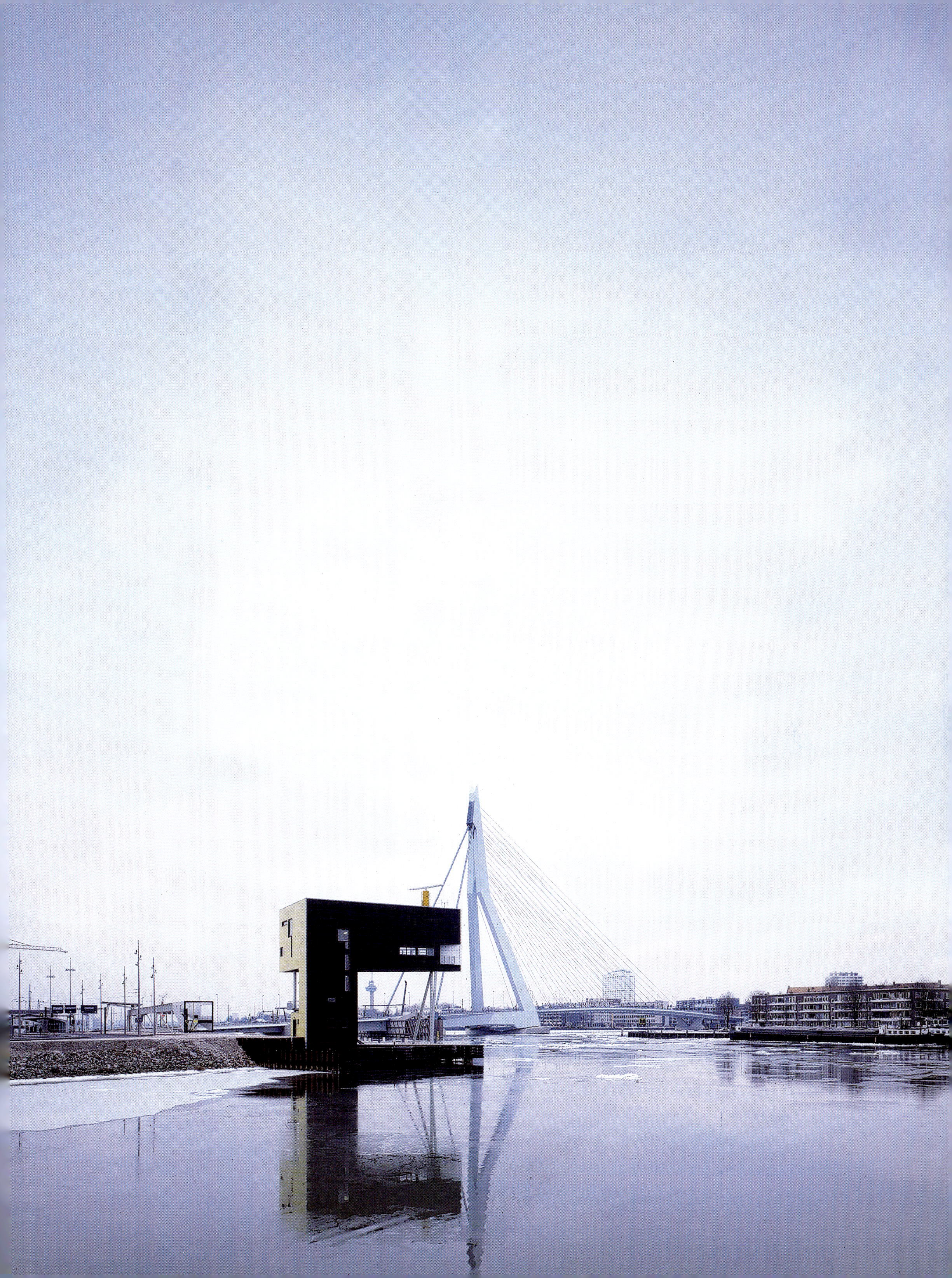

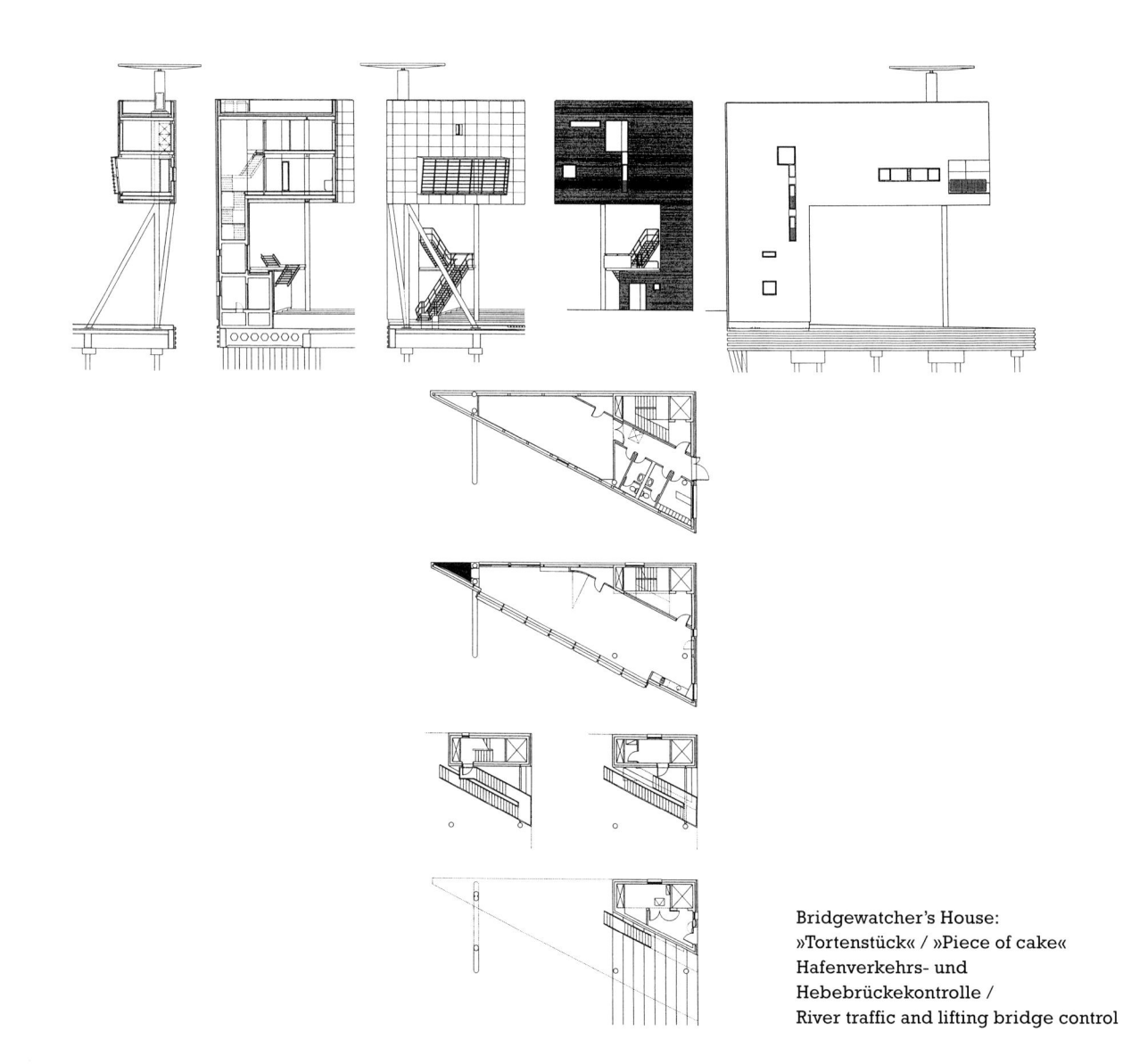

Bridgewatcher's House:
»Tortenstück« / »Piece of cake«
Hafenverkehrs- und
Hebebrückekontrolle /
River traffic and lifting bridge control

Bridgwatcher's House: Ansicht / Garten der fixierten Zahlen
Bridgewatcher's House: Elevation / Garden of Fixed Numbers

99 KOP VAN ZUID

Masse: Bridgewatcher's House als Ankerpunkt in der Stadt-/Hafenlandschaft
Mass: Bridgewatcher's house as anchorpoint in the urban/harbour landscape

Entwurfsmodell – rote Fassade
Skizzen – grüne Fassade
Gebäude – gelbe Fassade

Design model – red façade
Sketches – green façade
Built – yellow façade

101 KOP VAN ZUID

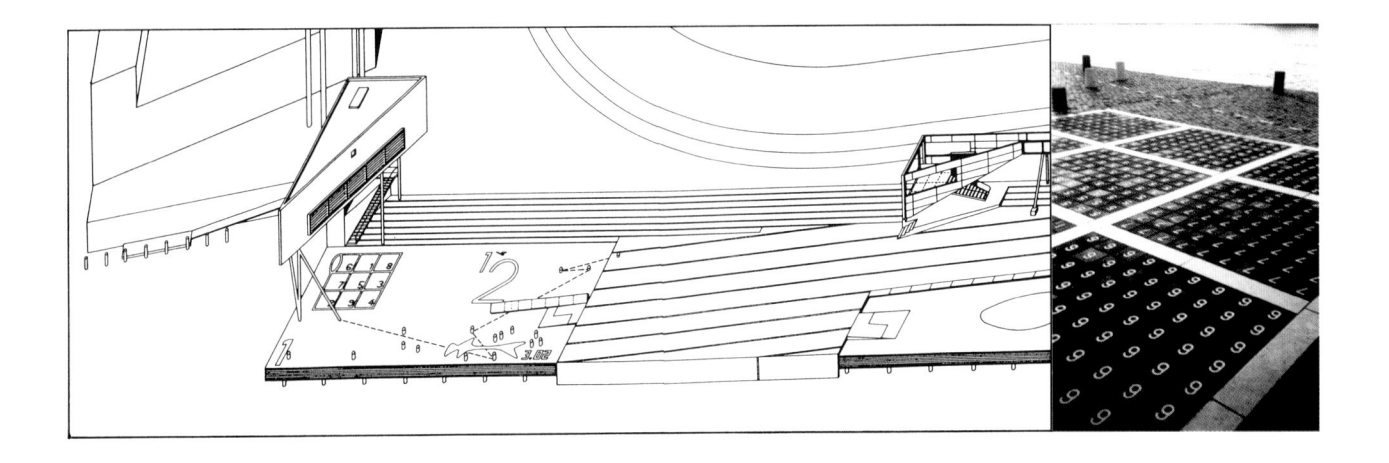

Inscribed Numbers   Garten der fixierten
Zahlen. Deaktivierte und
zerstreute Piernummern,
Höhe, Zahlenpuzzel
(die Antwort ist immer 15).
Garden of fixed numbers.
Deactivated and dispersed
pier numbers, height,
number puzzle
(the answer is always 15).

103　KOP VAN ZUID

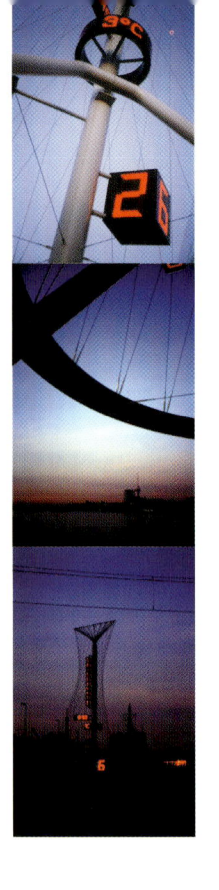

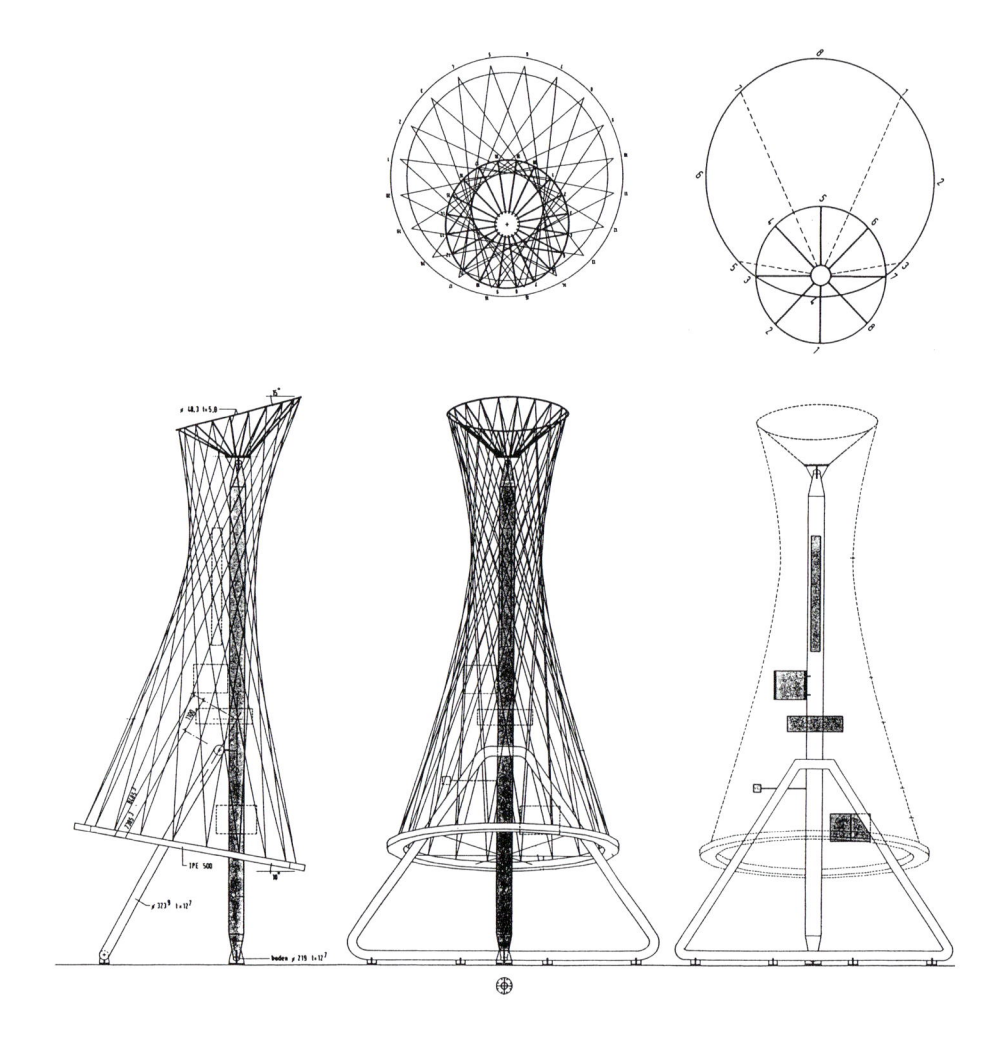

Moving Numbers

Turm der Elektronischen Zahlen
Zeit, Temperatur, Zufall, Null Herzschlag,
Weltpopulation. Vogelkäfig, Fliegender Ring

> Tower of Electronic Numbers
> Time, temperature, random,
> zero heartbeat, world population.
> Birdcage, flying ring

104 KOP VAN ZUID

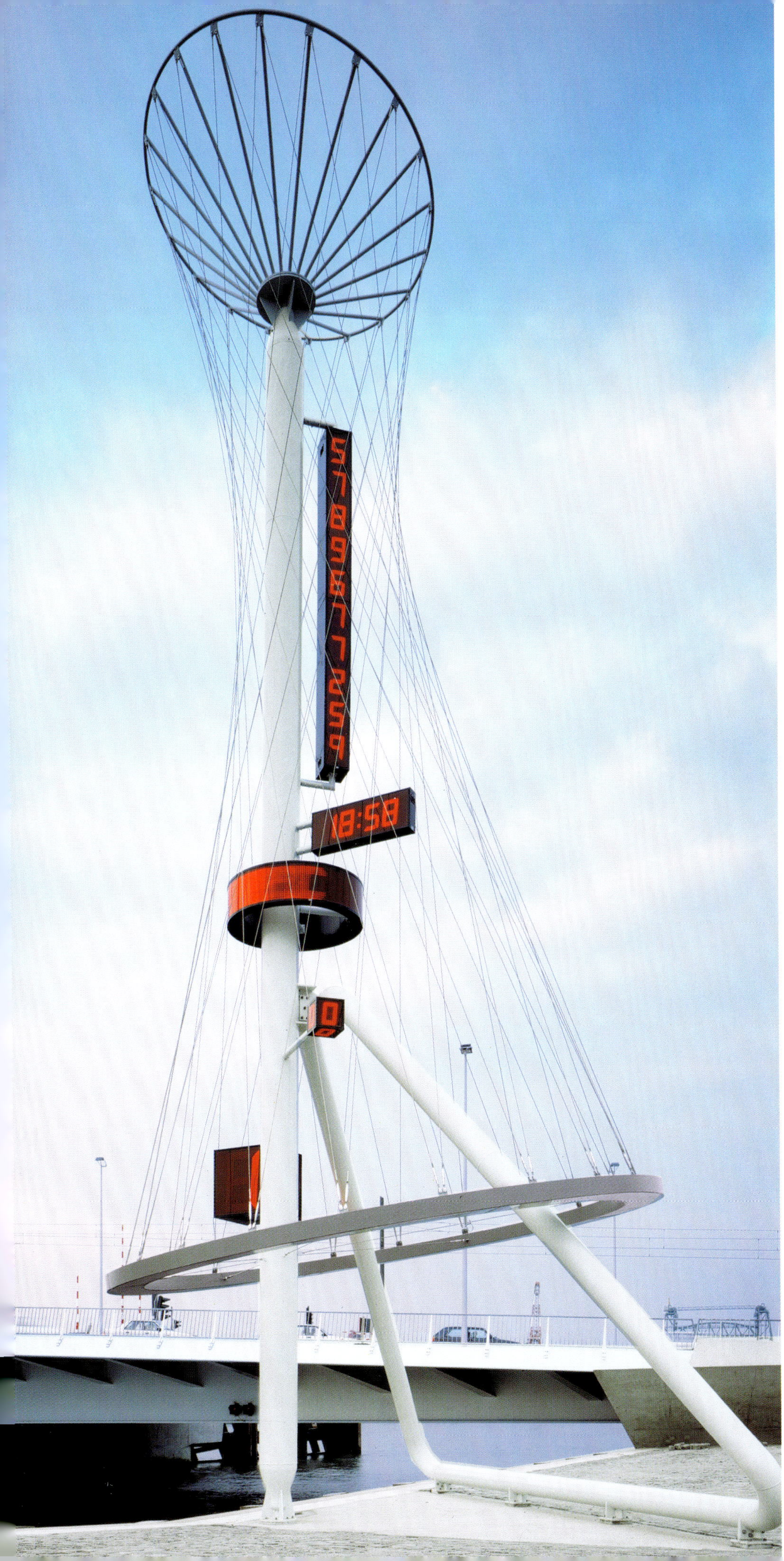
18:58

Neues Luxor Theater
New Luxor Theatre

Bauherr/Client: Stadt Rotterdam / City of Rotterdam
Standort/Location: Kop van Zuid, Rotterdam
Fertigstellung/Completion: 2000
Projektassistent/Project Assistant: Jim Yohe
Kontaktbüro/Contact: Bureau voor Bouwkunde
Statiker/Structural Engineer: Gemeentewerken Rotterdam
Techniker/Technician: Tebodin

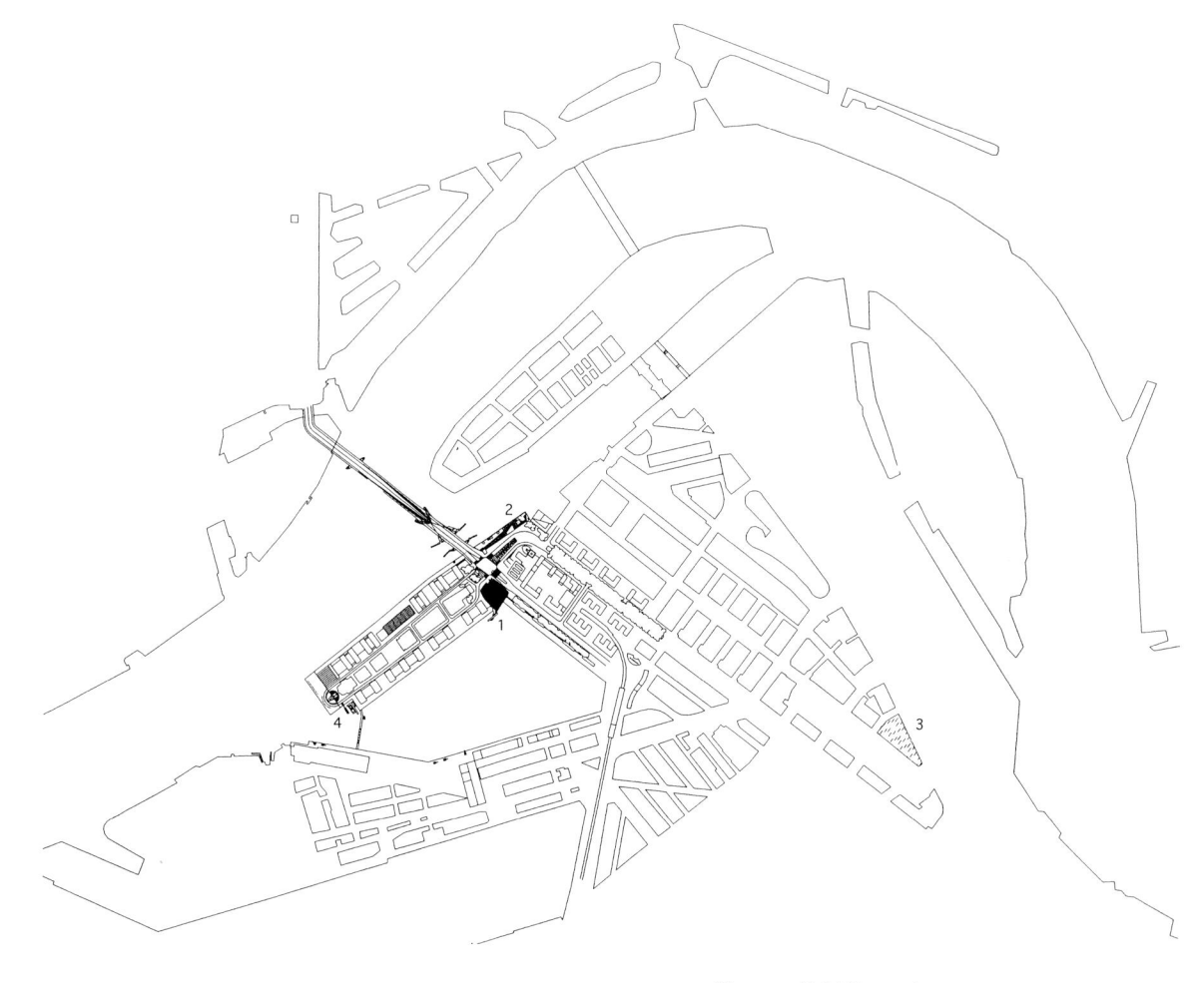

Kop van Zuid Rotterdam
1 Luxor, 2 Kai mit Bridgewatcher's House,
3 Albeda Schule, 4 Koninginnenhoofdarkade

Kop van Zuid Rotterdam
1 Luxor, 2 Quay with Bridgewatcher's house, 3 Albeda College,
4 Queens Head Quay

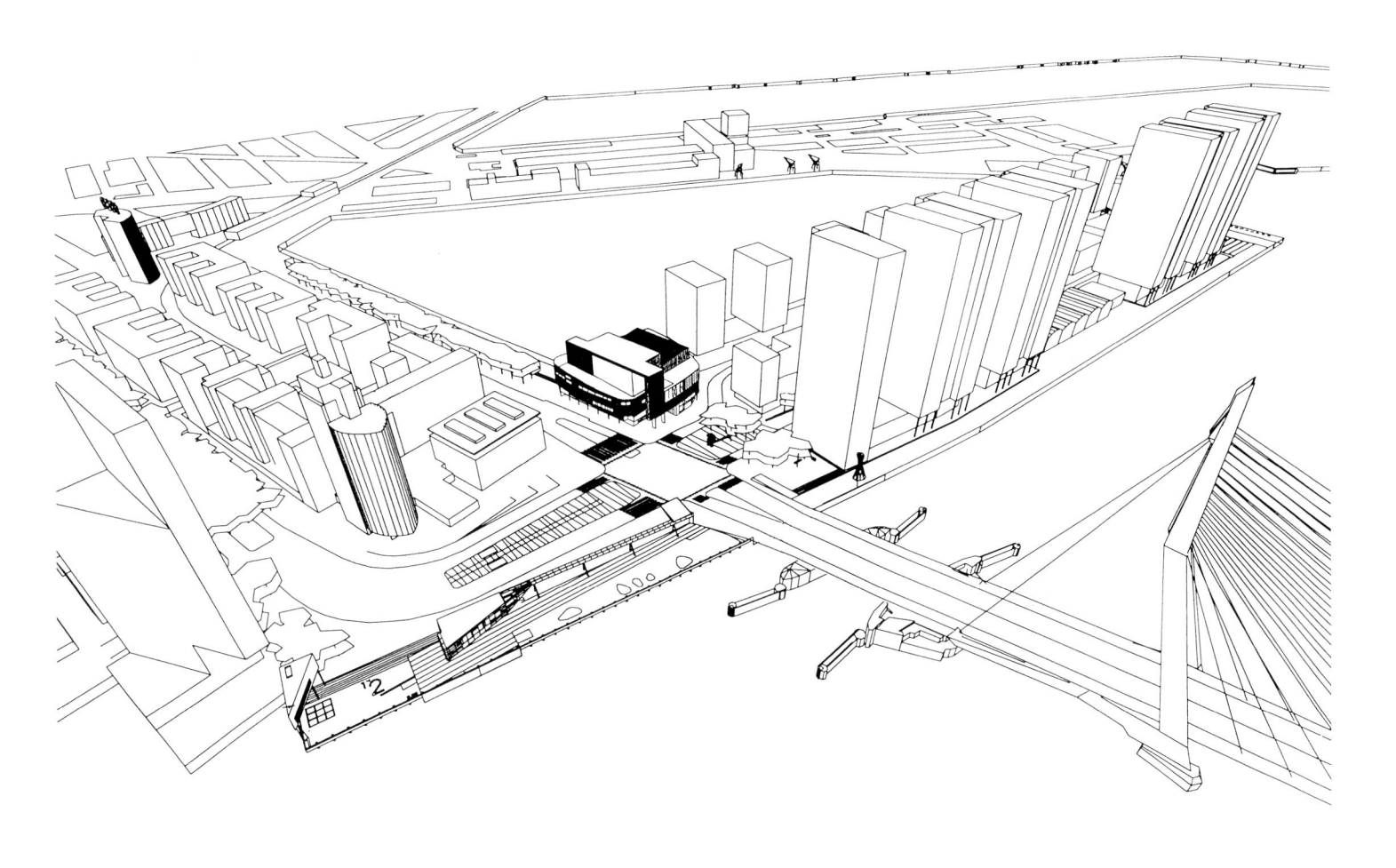

Das Neue Luxor Theater
im Kop van Zuid Rotterdam.
Wettbewerb 1. Preis 1996 –
Fertigstellung im Jahr 2000.
Das Neue Luxor bringt dem Kop van Zuid Urbanität, seine Lage verleiht dem Musiktheater mit 1.500 Sitzplätzen Bekanntheit und exzellente Zugänglichkeit. Ein 360° Grad Gebäude, eine simple, wahrnehmbare Form, eine spiralförmig einhüllende Fassade, sich für den Besucher in Richtung Stadt öffnend. Bühne und folglich auch Anlieferung sind im ersten Obergeschoß. Die Enge des Grundstücks erfordert die Absorption der Zufahrtsrampe für 18 m lange LKWs innerhalb des Gebäudevolumens. Das Dach der verschluckten Rampe wird zur Bewegungspromenade des Gebäudeinneren – eine sich entfaltende Sequenz vom Eingang bis zum Südfoyer. Farbe Rot – die spiralförmige, monochrom rote Fassade umarmt beim Eintreten in das Gebäude das Auditorium und gibt dieser inneren Halle der Illusion eine Atmosphäre von Luxus.

The New Luxor Theatre
Kop van Zuid Rotterdam.
Competition 1st prize 1996 –
opening 2000.
The New Luxor brings urbanity to the Kop van Zuid; the site gives prominence and accessibility to the 1,500 audience musical theatre.
A 360° hinge building, a simple recognisable form, a wrapping spiral façade opening at the city-facing entrance.
Stage and therefore delivery are at first floor level. Site limits require the absorption of the ramp for 18-meter lorries within the building volume. The roof of the swallowed ramp becomes movement promenade within – an unfolding sequence from entrance to south foyer. Red – the spiralling monochrome façade on entering the building embraces the auditorium, its colour pervading and giving an atmosphere of luxury to this inner hall of illusion.

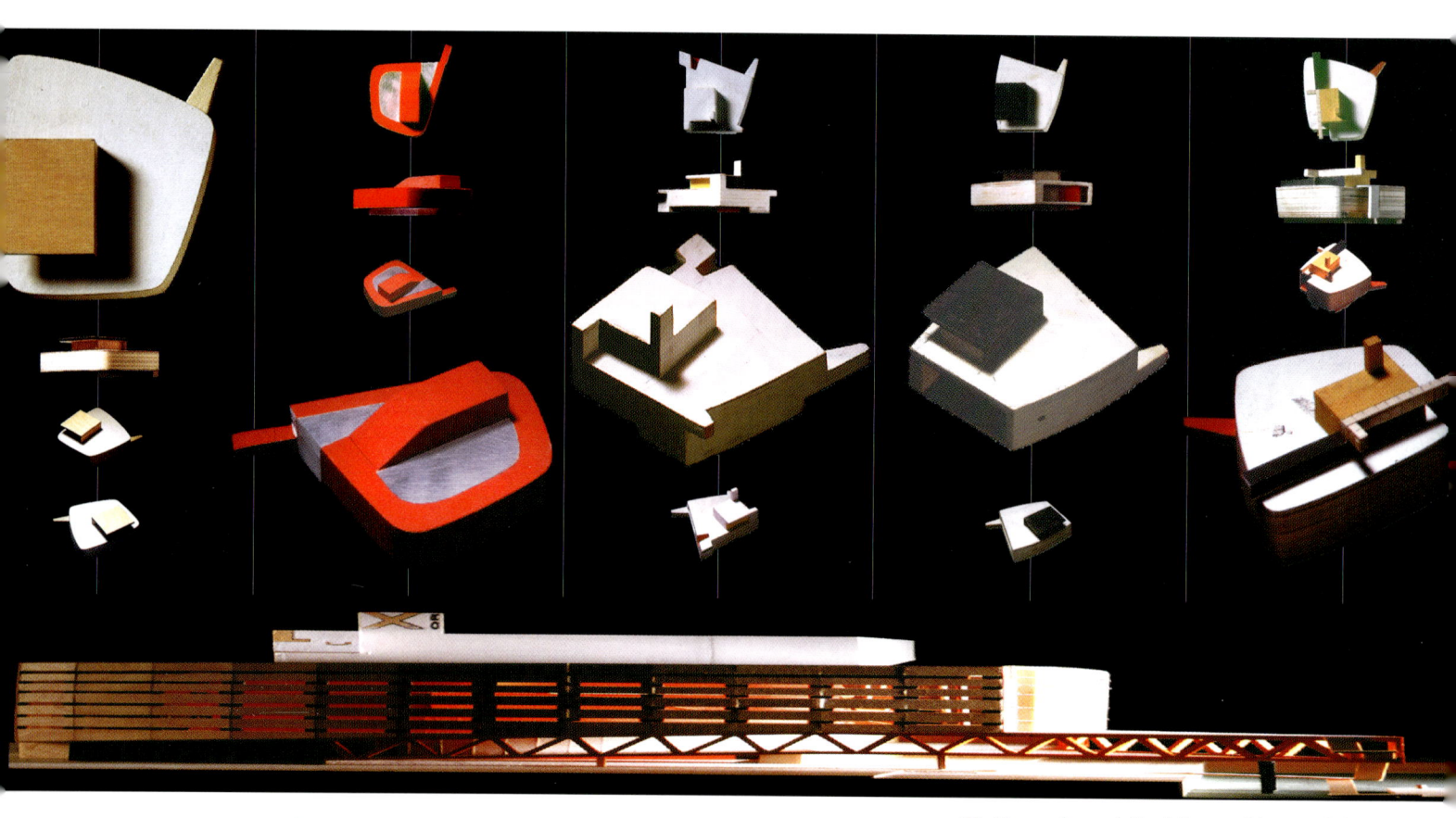

Wettbewerbsmodelle / Competition models

Omnia Publica Ligna Theatra ... Vitruvius

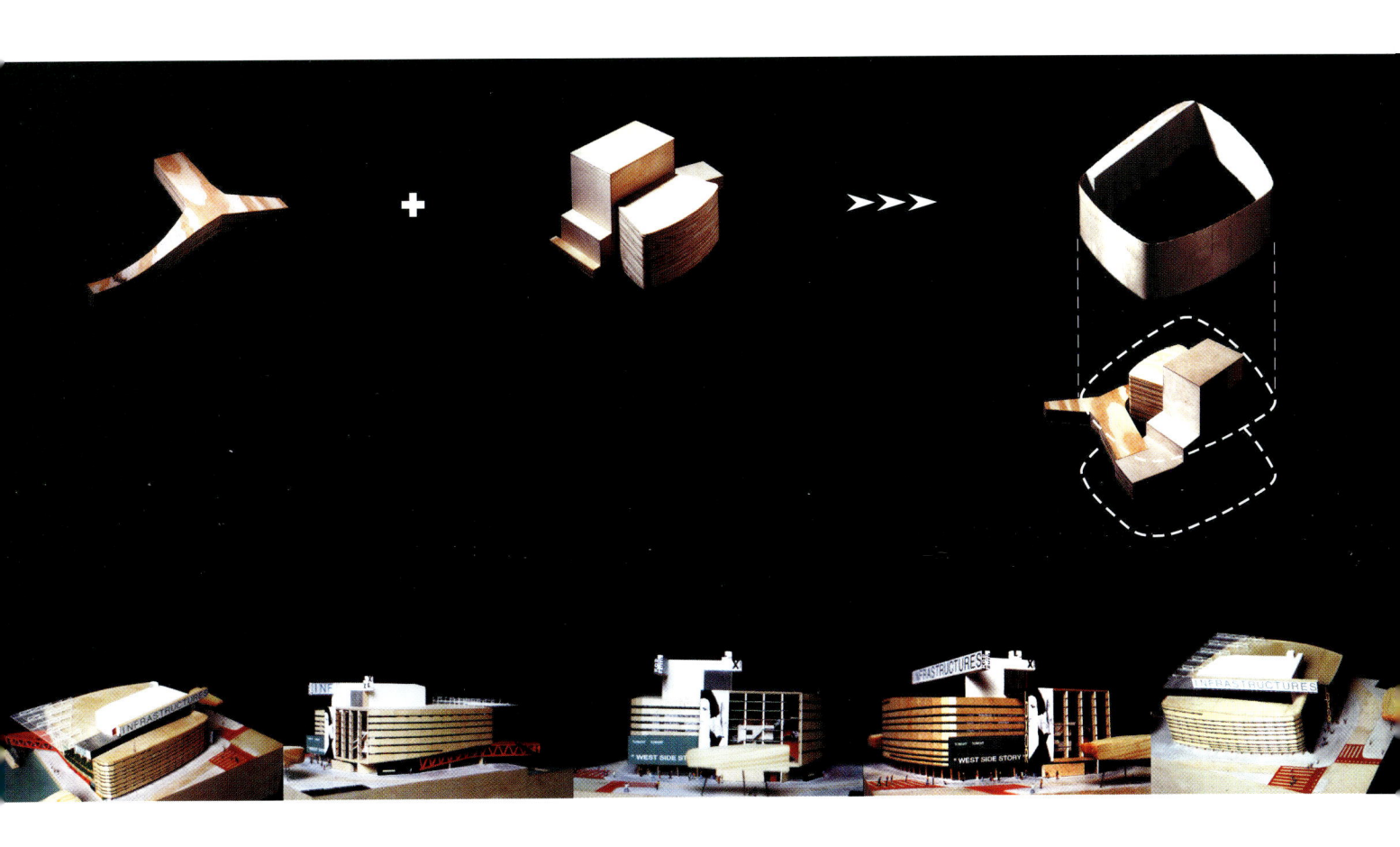

Gebäude schluckt Rampe
Die Absorption der Anlieferrampe ist der Schlüssel zur Organisation des Neuen Luxor. Aus den Wendekreisen der 18,5 Meter langen LKWs wurde eine optimale, dreidimensionale Rampenform entwickelt. Rampe und gegebene Theatergeometrie sind dann »eng zusammengepackt« innerhalb der kontinuierlichen Fassade.

Building swallows ramp
Delivery ramp absorption is the key to the New Luxor organisation. From the turning circles of 18.5 meter lorries, an optimal three dimensional ramp form is developed. Ramp and given theatre geometry are then »close packed« within the continuous façade.

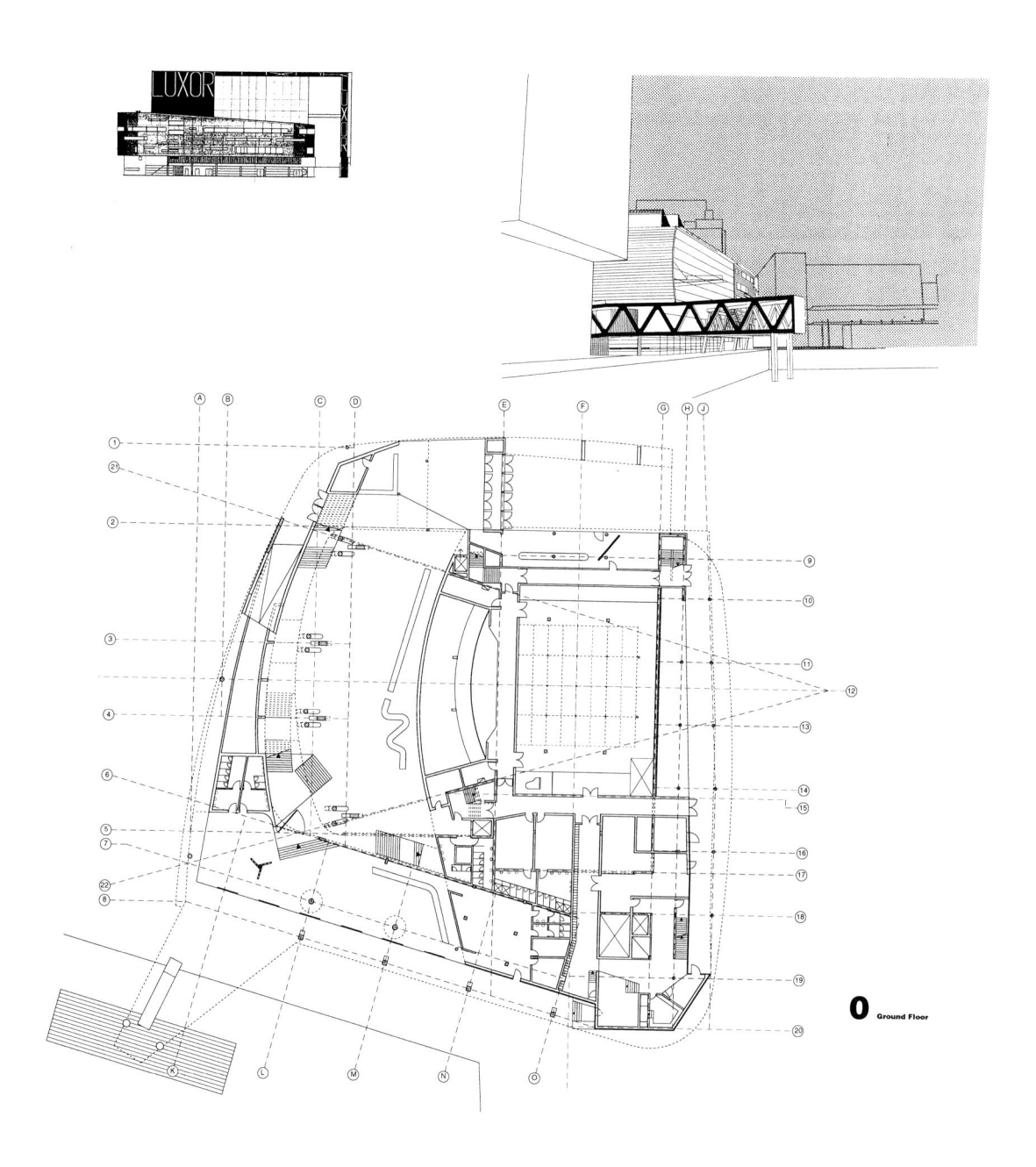

Erdgeschoß – Eingang, Garderobe, Café
Rechts: 1. Obergeschoß – Zuschauerraum,
Promenadenrampe – Bühne Anlieferung/
Verladung

Ground floor – Entrance, cloaks, café
Right: 1st floor – Auditorium,
processional ramp – Stage delivery/
loading

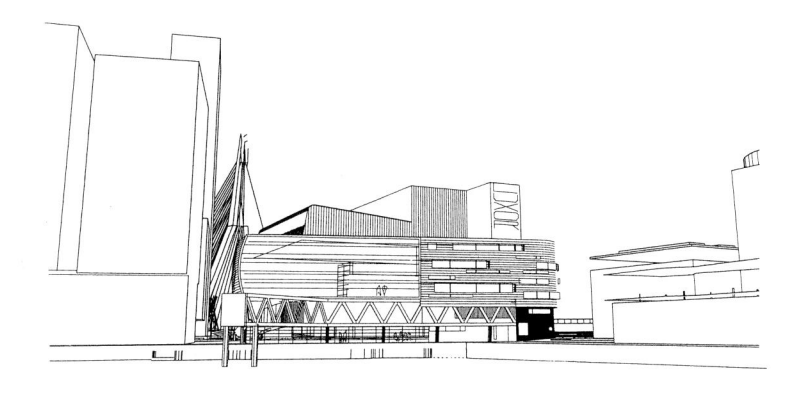

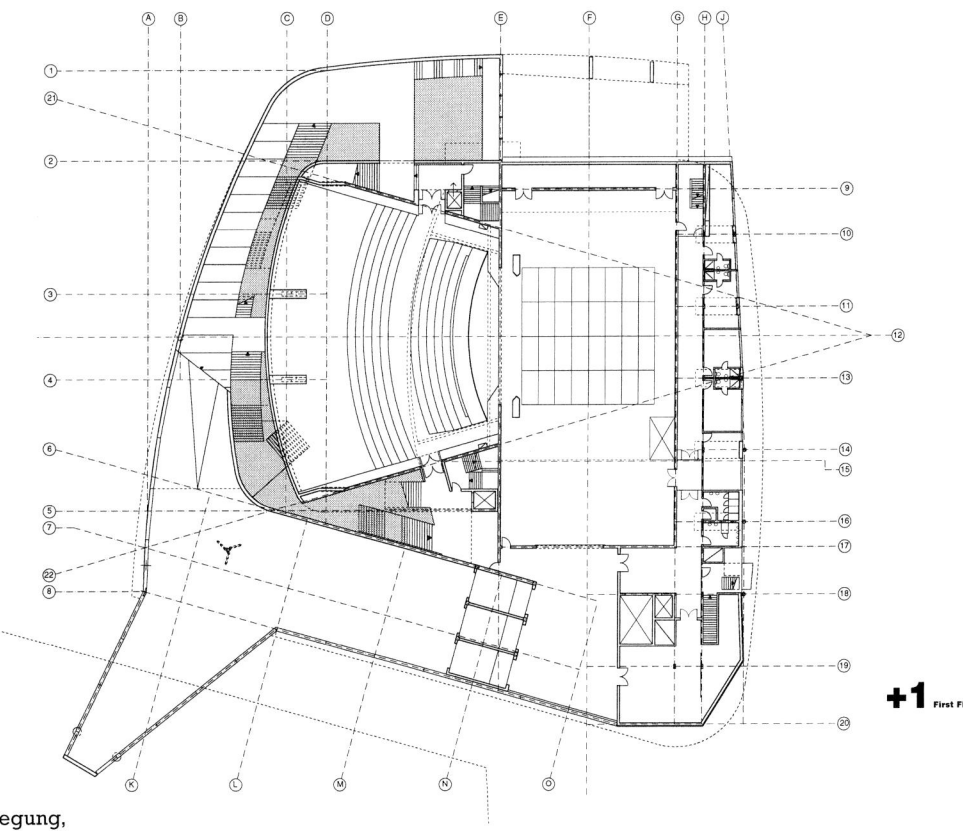

Sequenz
Ein Theaterfoyer ist ein Raum der Bewegung, ein Fluß von Besuchern, passend zu der durch das Grundstück vorgeschriebenen Bewegung – ein Vektor vom Eingang des Landungsplatzes zum südorientierten Rheinhafenausblick. Diese Bewegung reflektiert die der Lieferwagen, daher ist es logisch, das Rampendach als »Promenade« durch das Gebäude zu nutzen.

Sequence
A theatre foyer is a space of movement, a flow of visitors here matched to site prescribed movement – a vector from landing square entrance to south oriented Rijnhaven views. This movement echoes that of delivery lorries, it is logical therefore to utilise the ramp roof as »promenade« through the building.

NEW LUXOR THEATRE

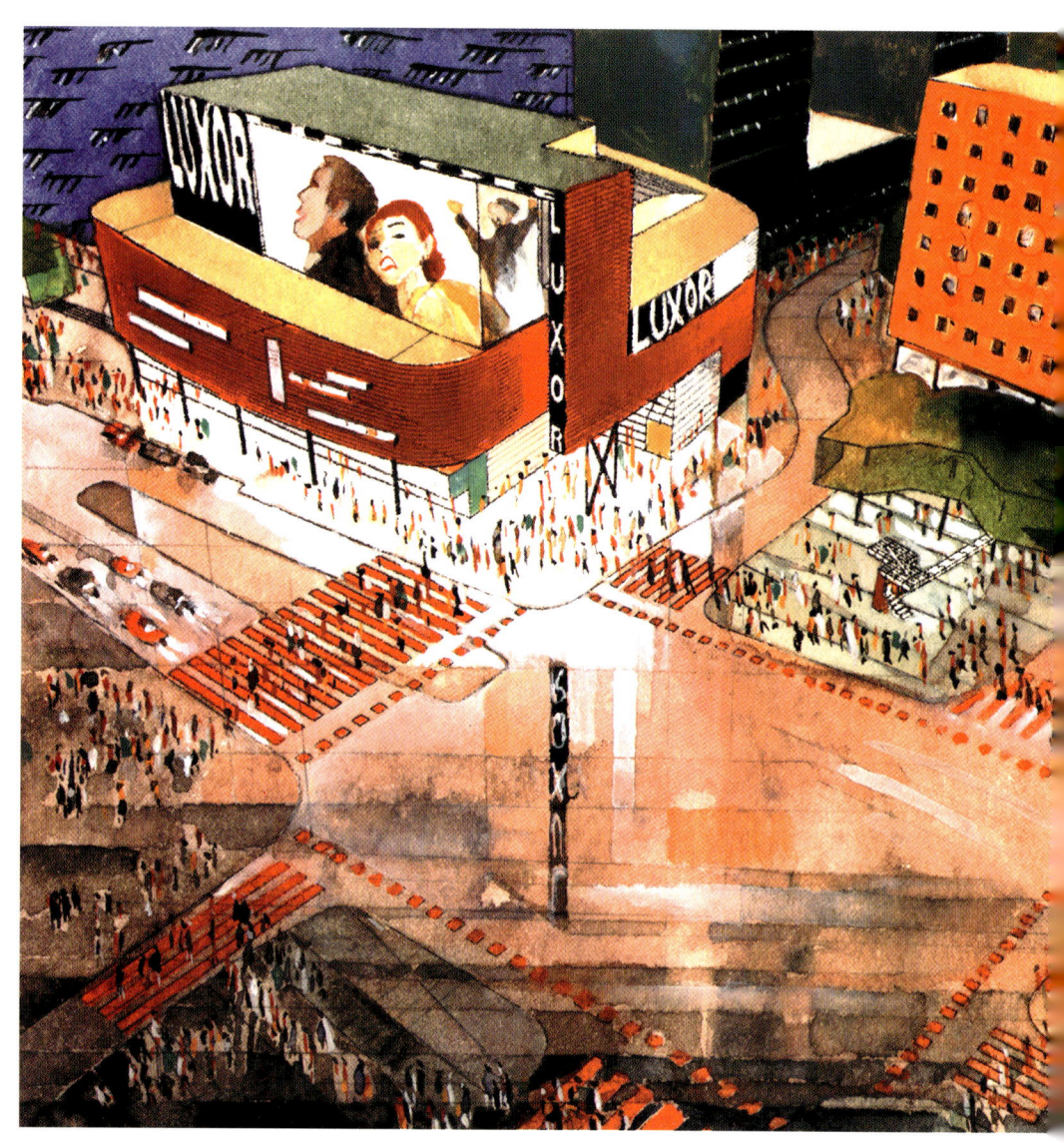

Opening night

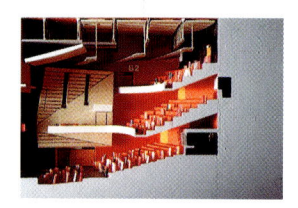

Auditorium:
Wettbewerbsmodell /
Competition model

112 NEUES LUXOR THEATER

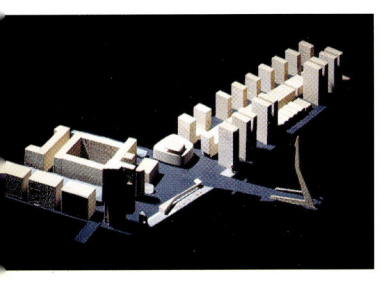

Image
Tomatenrot einwickelnde Fassade – ein Thema, das schon durch den »gigantischen roten Zebrastreifen« des Landungsplatzes angekündigt wird.
Monochromes Rot – inmitten des Zuschauerraumes, auf den segelähnlichen Akustikpaneelen wieder zu finden, ein seitlicher Abschluß, der den Zuschauerraum mit der Bühne verbindet, um eine »intime Raumatmosphäre« zu schaffen.

Image
Tomato red wrapping façade – a theme already announced by the »giant red zebra crossing« of the landing square.
Monochrome red – is, within the auditorium, found on the sail-like acoustic panels, a side enclosure linking audience and stage to produce a »single intimate room atmosphere«.

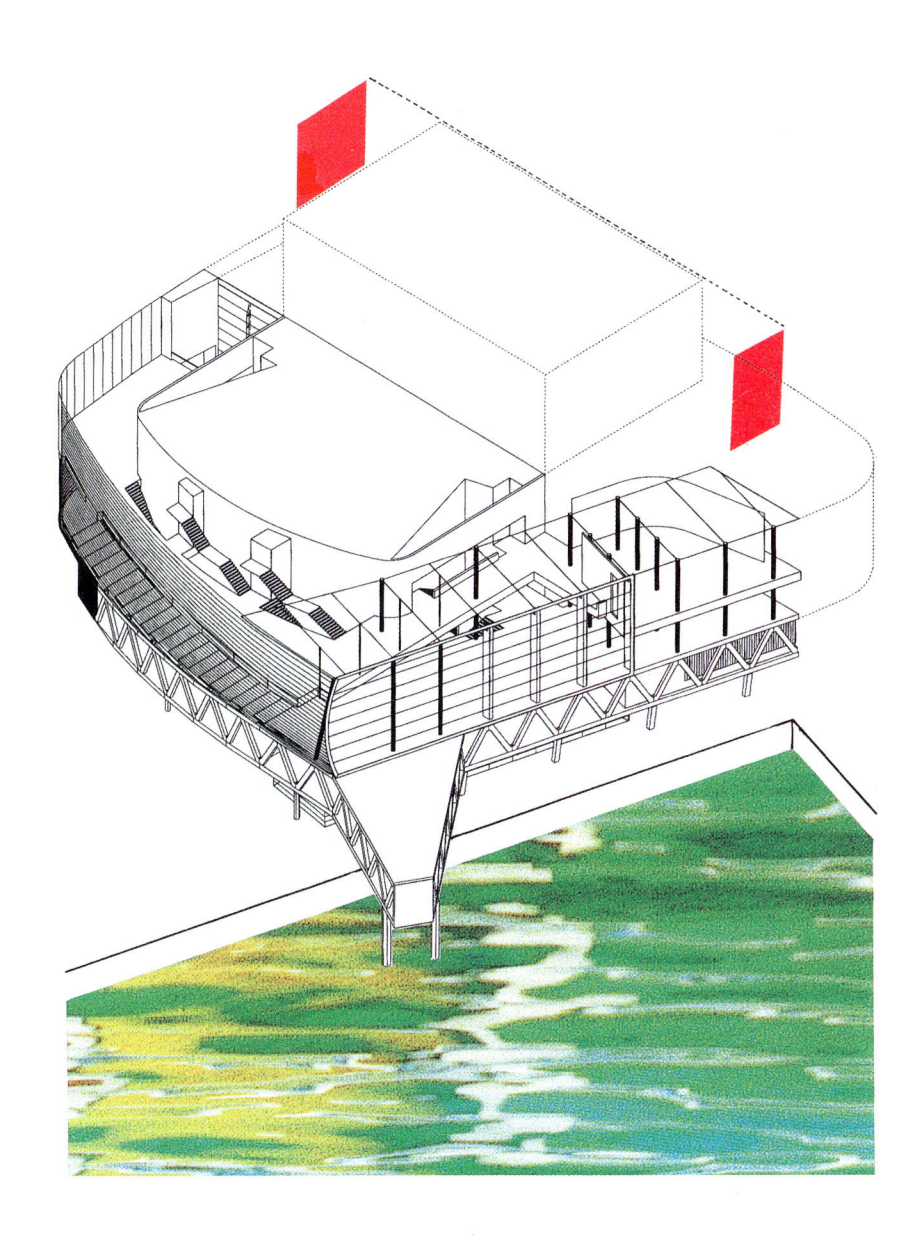

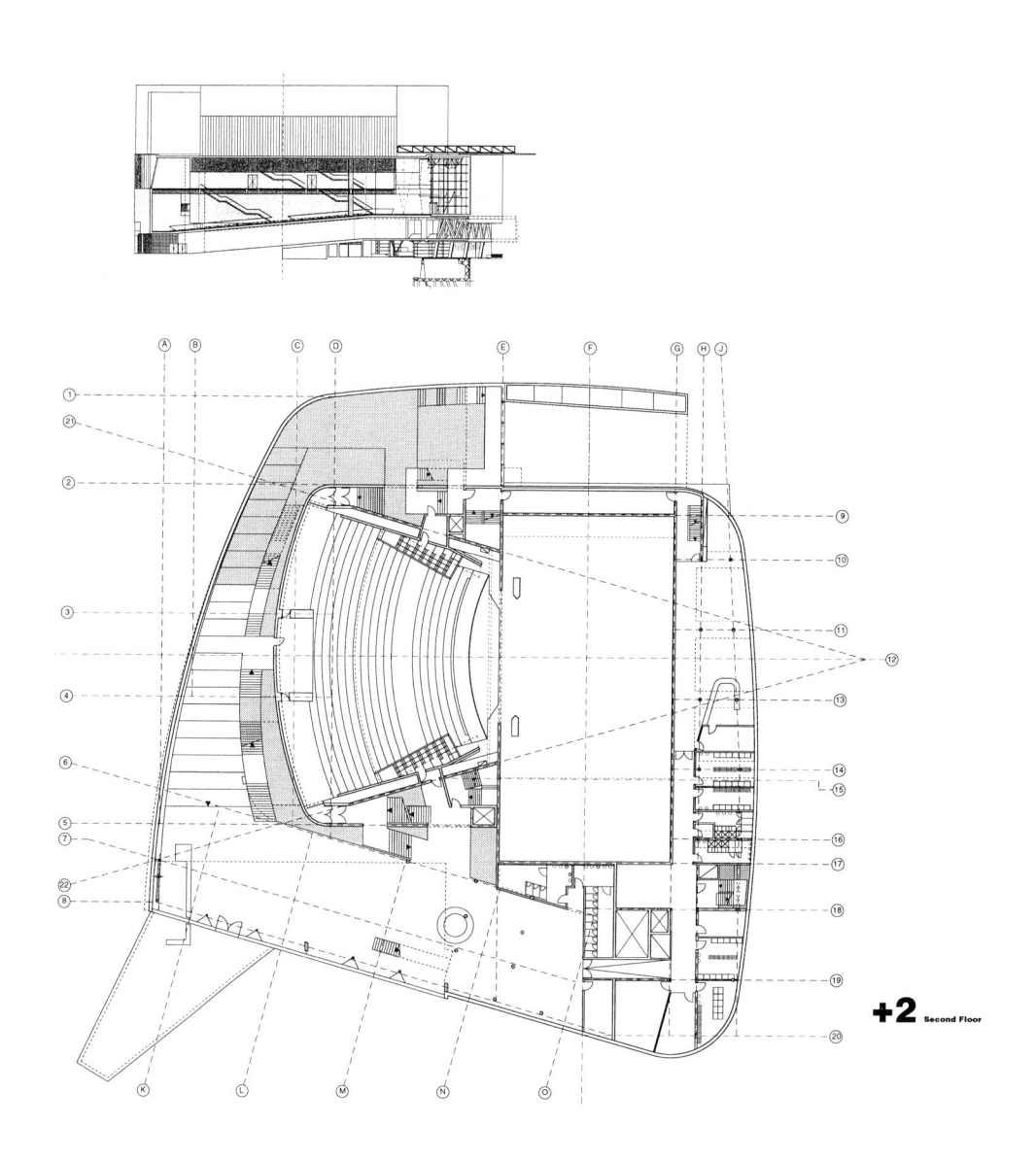

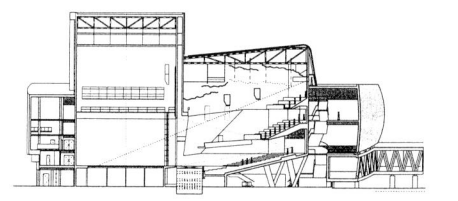

+2 – Süd Foyer
Rechts: +4 – Balkonniveau – Obere Foyers
+2 – South foyer
Right: +4 – Balcony level – Upper foyers

114 NEUES LUXOR THEATER

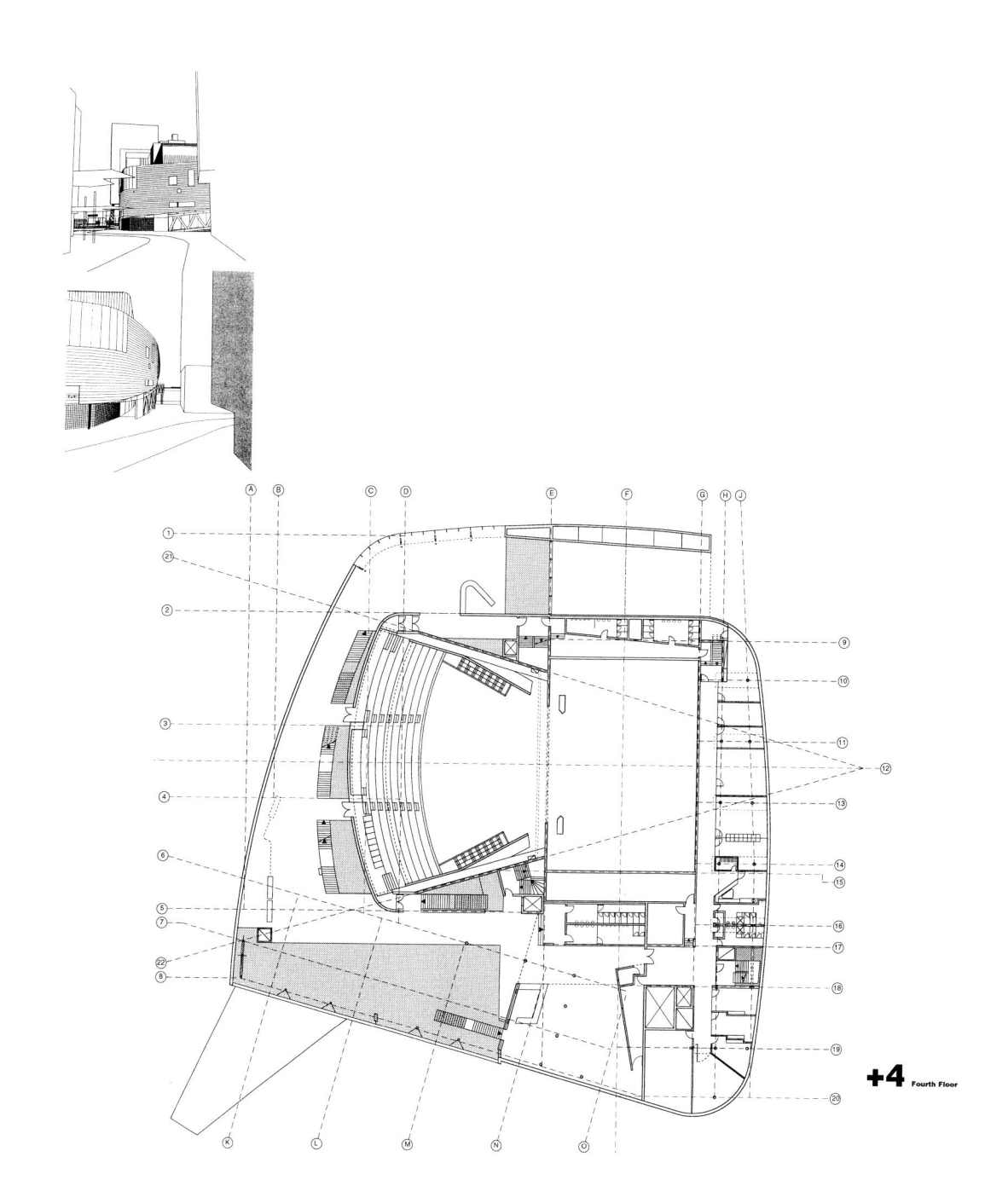

Die Intention dieses Entwurfs ist es, den präzise vorgegebenen Theaterfunktionen eine klare Form zu geben, einen neuen Akteur auf die gleichermaßen präzise definierte, urbane Bühne zu projizieren.

> The intention of this design is to give clear form to the precisely prescribed theatre functions, to project a new actor on to the equally precisely defined urban stage.

Brink-Viertel
Brink Centre

Bauherr/Client: ING
Vastgoed
Ontwikkeling
Standort/Location:
Bahnhof und Markt /
Station and market
Hengelo, NL
Fertigstellung/
Completion: 1999
Projektassistent/
Project Assistant:
Axel Kempers
Kontaktbüro/Contact:
Bureau voor
Bouwkunde
Statiker/
Structural Engineer:
ABT, Velp
Techniker/Technician:
De Boer en Post

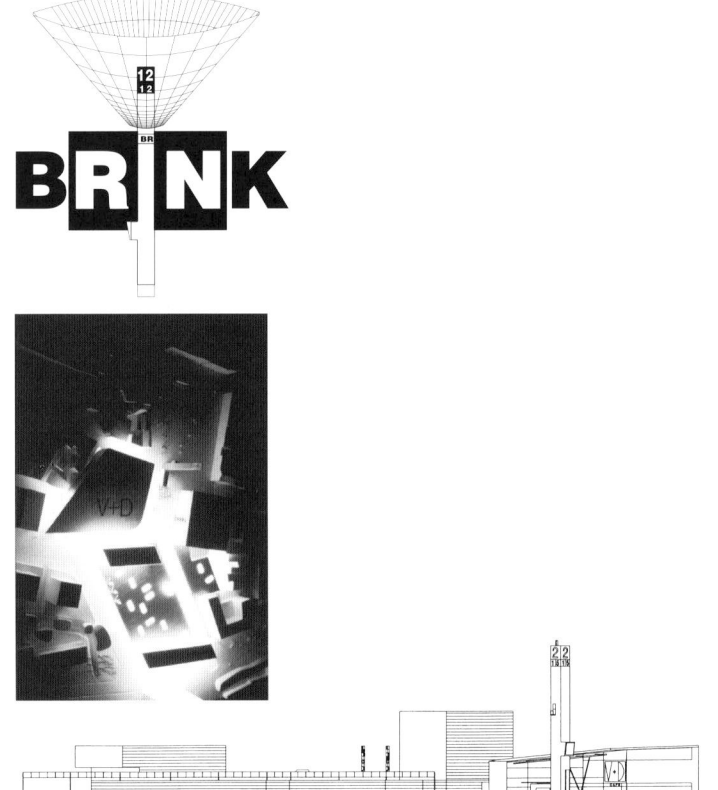

Wettbewerb / Competition 1995

Brink-Viertel Hengelo,
Wettbewerb, 1. Preis 1995.
Hengelo – eine Industriestadt im Osten von Holland, nach der Kriegszerstörung rationalisiert, ist nun der Ort für weitere katalytische Injektionen.
Die Verbindung vom Marktplatz zum Bahnhofsplatz entsteht durch eine neue Einkaufspassage. Wie St. Markus in Venedig ist der doppelte Platz (Brink und Markt) durch einen Turm gelenkig verbunden – dem Elektronischen Kampanile. Eine ähnliche ikonische Funktion in der horizontalen Dimension hat das »pneumatische Zigarrendach« der Passage. Einkaufen ist in zwei unterschiedliche Typologien aufgeteilt: das Kaufhaus, ein metallischer Monolith mit überhängender und gefalteter Dachebene, und die horizontale Einkaufsplatte. Darüber, auf dem Dach, befinden sich zwei »buchstützenähnliche« Apartmentblocks, die diesem Einkaufen eine urbane Präsenz verleihen. Materialität und Masse übernehmen hier den Vorrang gegenüber Transparenz, den unzusammenhängenden Kontext eher verankernd als auflösend.

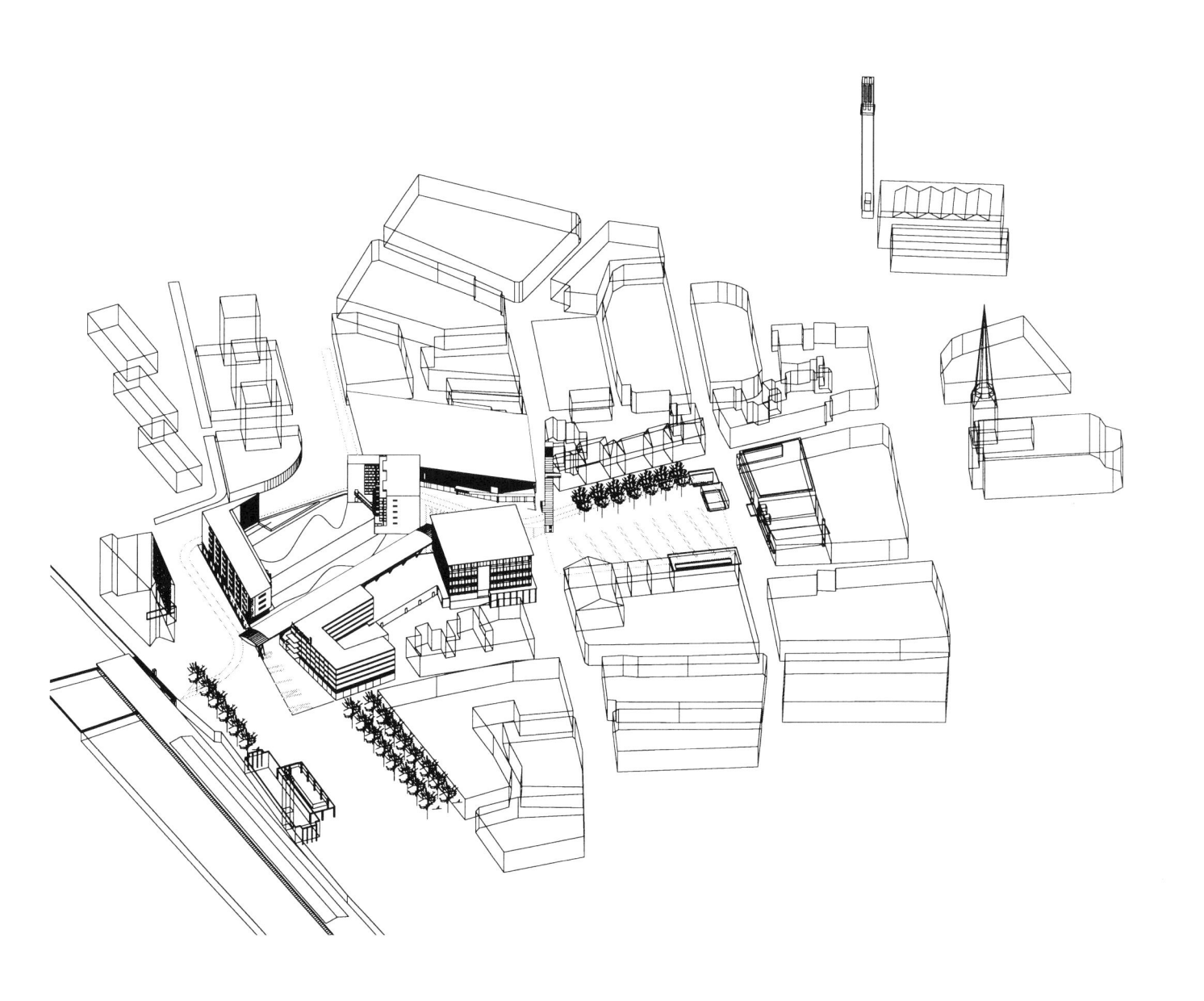

Brink Centre Hengelo,
competition, 1st prize 1995
Hengelo – an industrial city in the east of Holland rationalised after wartime destruction, now the site of further catalytic injection.
The connection from Market Square to Station Square is via a new Shopping Passage. Like St. Marks in Venice the double Square (Brink and Market) is linked and hinged by a tower – the Electronic Campanile. Performing a similarly iconic function in the horizontal dimension is the »Inflated Cigar Roof« of the passage. Shopping is divided into two distinct typologies: the department store, a metallic monolith with an overhanging and folded roof plain, and the horizontal shopping slab. On top and giving this shopping an urban presence are two »bookend-like« apartment blocks. Materiality and mass here take precedence over transparency, anchoring rather than dissolving the discoherent context.

Brink Square

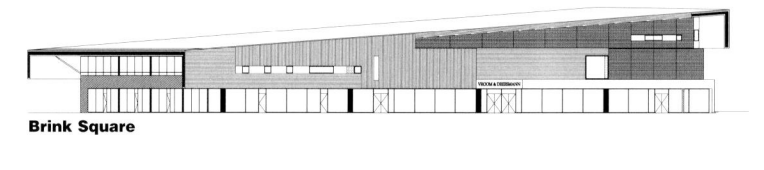

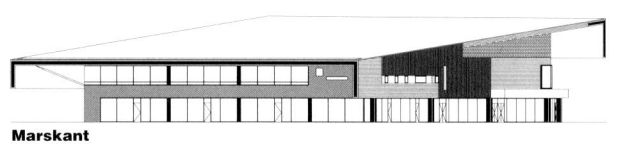

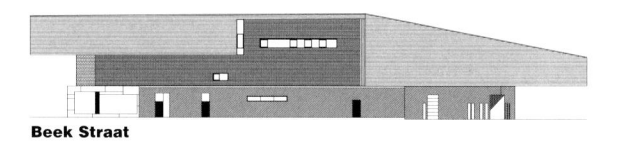

Marskant

Beek Straat

Kaufhaus mit gefaltetem Dach /
Department store with folded roof

UG / Basement floor

EG / Ground floor

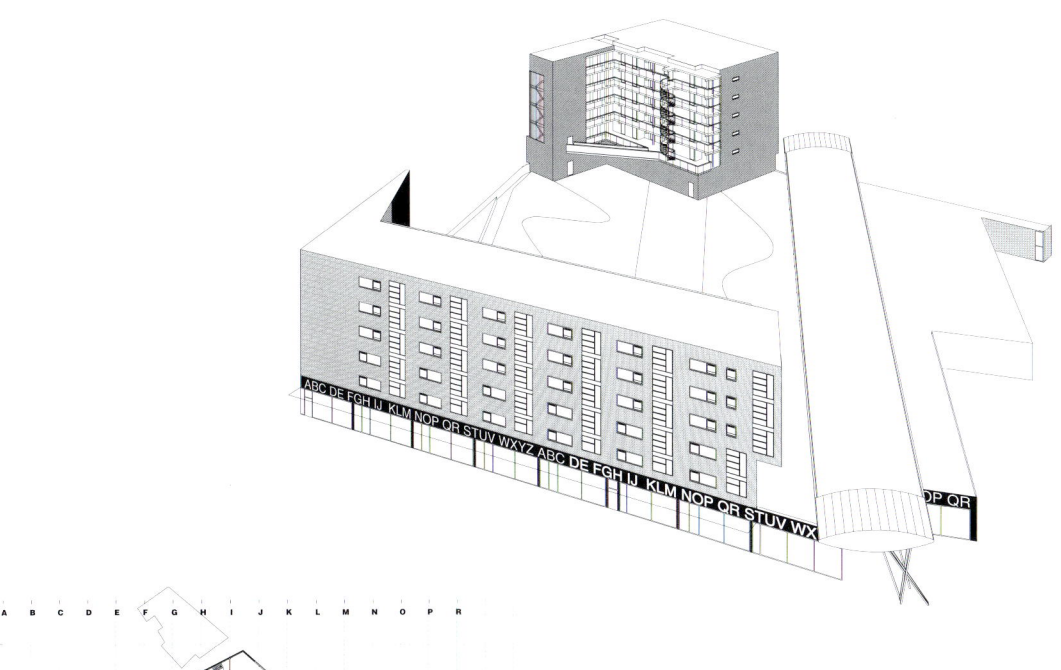

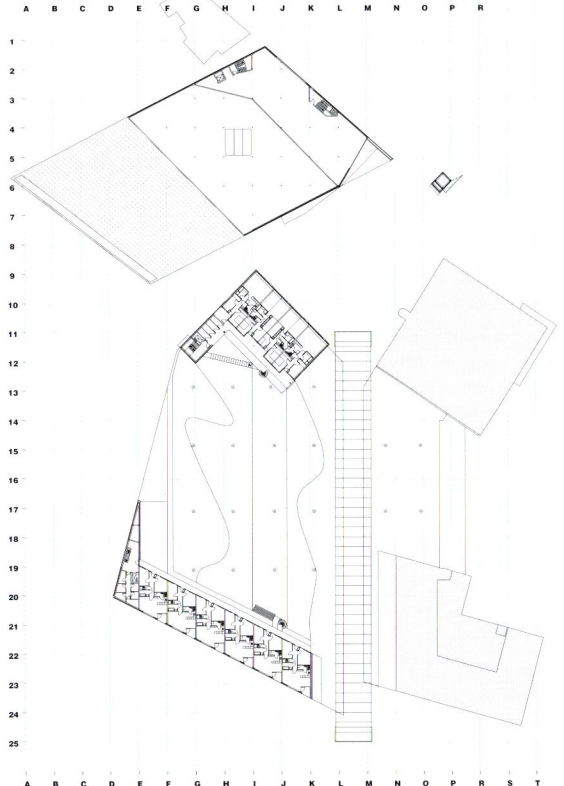

Marskant
Wohnen Ansicht + 3D / Housing elevation + 3D

OG / Upper floor

Grundrisse / Plans
UG: 400 PKWs / Basement: 400 cars
EG: Passage, Läden / 1st floor: passage, shops
OG: Wohnungen, Kaufhaus / Upper floor: apartments, department store

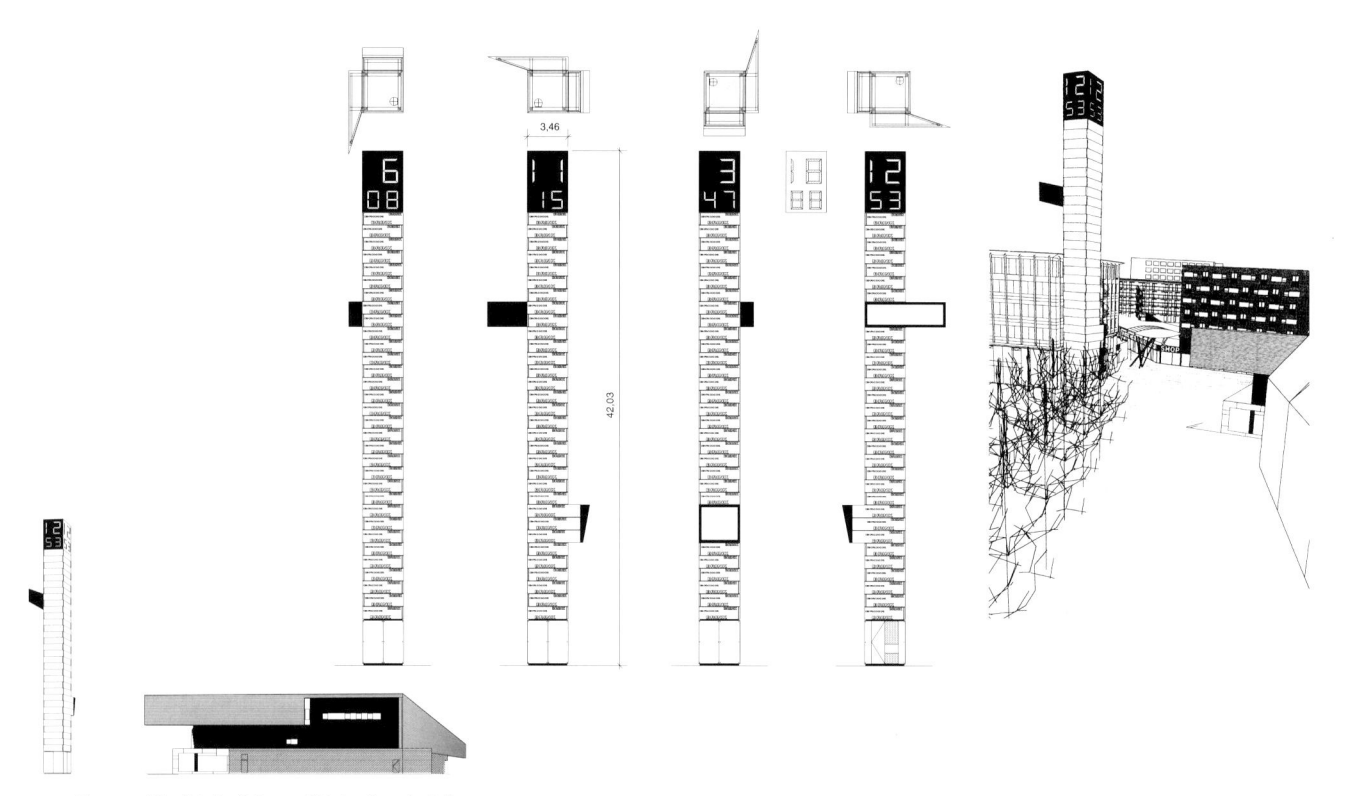

Turm – Ein Licht/Masse/Licht-Sandwich
Vorgefertigte Paneele, Glaslaternensokkel, LED-illuminierte Spitze

Tower – A light/mass/light sandwich
Precast panels, glass lantern base, LED-illuminated top

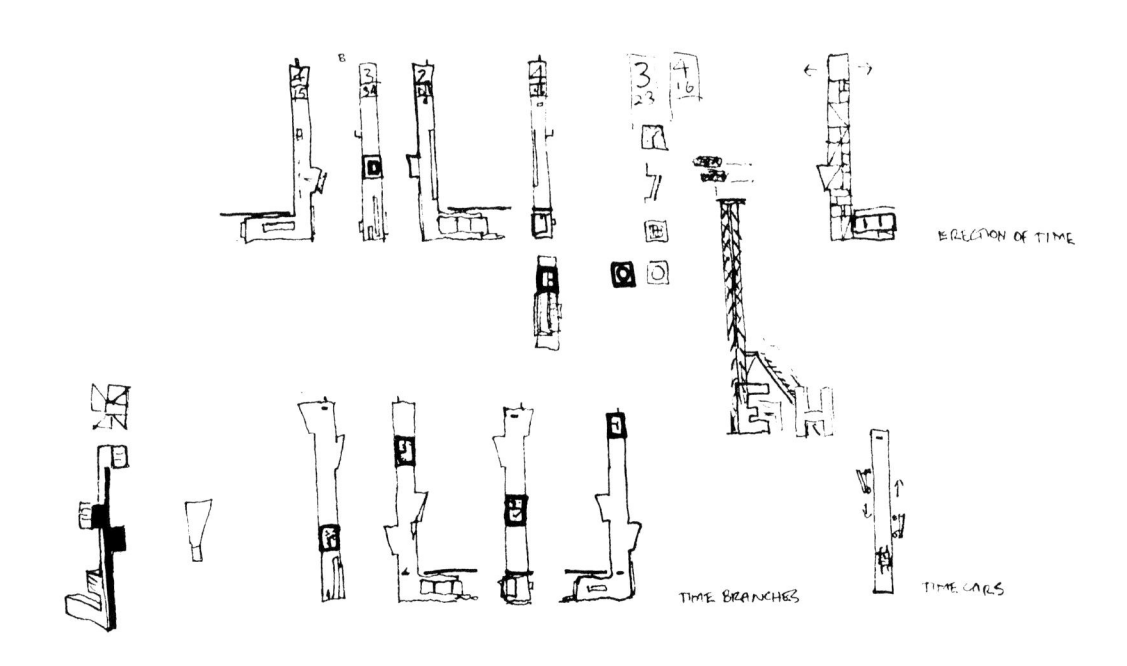

121 BRINK CENTRE

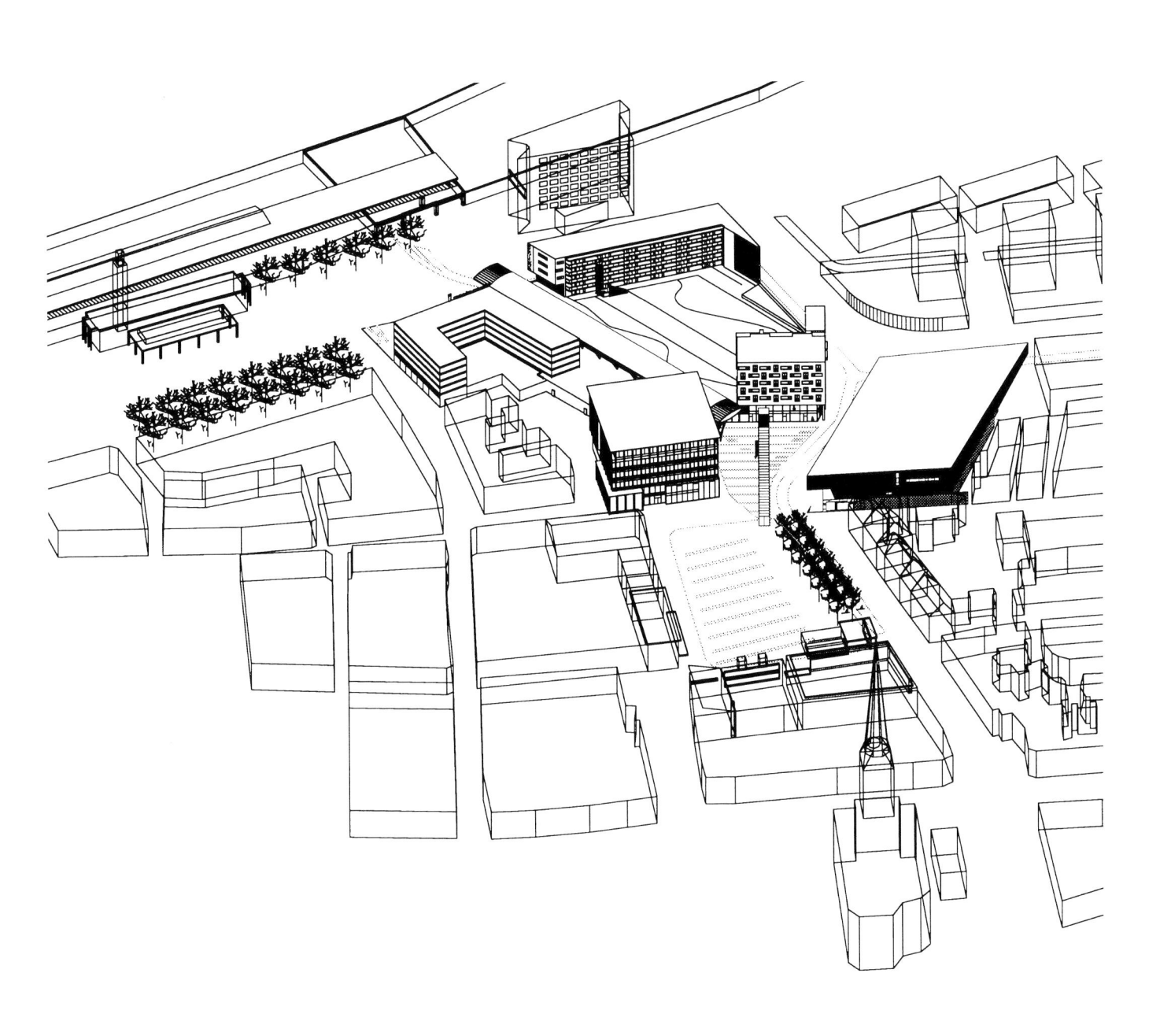

Biographien
Biographies

Peter Wilson · Julia Bolles

Peter L. Wilson wurde 1950 in Melbourne/Australien geboren. Er studierte Architektur an der University of Melbourne und arbeitete im Büro von Robin Boyd, bevor er sein Studium an der Architectural Association in London mit dem AA Diploma Prize 1974 abschloß. Von 1974 bis 1976 war er Assistent von Elia Zenghelis und dann von 1978 bis 1988 Diploma Unit Master an der AA.

Peter Wilson ist der Autor folgender Bücher: *The Villa Auto* AA 1980, *Shipshapes and Bridgebuildings* AA 1984, *The Clandeboye Report* AA 1985, *Informing the Object* AA 1986, *Western Objects and Eastern Fields* AA 1989.

Peter Wilson war Gastdozent an der Sommerakademie Berlin 1987, Workshop for Architecture and Urbanism Tokio 1987, Berlage Akademie Amsterdam 1994–1995 und Sommerakademie Barcelona 1996. 1994–1996 war er Gastprofessor an der Kunsthochschule Weißensee Berlin.

Julia B. Bolles-Wilson wurde 1948 in Münster/Westfalen geboren. Sie studierte Architektur an der Universität Karlsruhe, u. a. am Lehrstuhl von Egon Eiermann und Ottokar Uhl. Nach dem Diplom 1976 arbeitete sie im Büro Prof. Karl-Heinz Götz. 1978 erhielt sie ein DAAD-Stipendium für ein Postgraduierten-Studium bei Elia Zenghelis und Rem Koolhaas an der Architectural Association in London. Von 1981 bis 1986 war sie Dozentin für Architectural Studies an der Chelsea School of Art London. Julia Bolles-Wilson ist gegenwärtig Professorin an der FH Münster.

Bolles + Wilson haben in Architekturwettbewerben und für ihr gebautes Werk viele nationale und internationale Preise gewonnen, u. a. den Förderpreis des Deutschen Stahlbaus 1976 (Julia Bolles und Hans Stadler), den 1. Preis im Shinken shiku Wettbewerb 1989, den Deutschen Architekturpreis (Anerkennung) für Kita Frankfurt/Griesheim und die Stadtbücherei Münster und die Goldmedaille 1994 der Japanischen Architektenkammer für Suzuki House. Ausstellungen: Biennale in Venedig 1980, AA London 1980/84/89, Aedes Berlin 1989/97, Storefront New York 1990, Centre d'Architecture Bordeaux 1990, Westfälischer Kunstverein Münster 1993, GA Gallery Tokio 1994, Phillipe Uzzan Galerie Paris 1995, Biennale in Venedig 1996.

Peter L. Wilson was born in 1950 in Melbourne, Australia. He studied architecture at the University of Melbourne and worked in the office of Robin Boyd before completing his studies at the Architectural Association in London (AA Diploma Prize 1974). He was assistant to Elia Zenghelis from 1974–1976 and then from 1978–1988 Diploma Unit Master at the AA.

Peter Wilson is the author of: *The Villa Auto* AA 1980, *Shipshapes and Bridgebuildings* AA 1984, *The Clandeboye Report* AA 1985, *Informing the Object* AA 1986, *Western Objects and Eastern Fields* AA 1989.

Peter Wilson has also been a visiting critic at Summer Academy Berlin 1987, Workshop for Architecture and Urbanism Tokyo 1987, Berlage Academy Amsterdam 1994–95 and Summer Academy Barcelona 1996. He was from 1994–96 a visiting Professor at the Kunsthochschule Berlin Weissensee.

Julia B. Bolles-Wilson was born in Münster, Westfalen in 1948. She studied architecture at the University of Karlsruhe in the Department of Egon Eiermann and Ottokar Uhl. After her diploma in 1976, she worked in the office of Professor Karl-Heinz Götz. In 1978 she received a DAAD-scholarship for postgraduate studies at the AA in London with Elia Zenghelis and Rem Koolhaas. From 1981 to 1986 she taught at Chelsea School of Art London. Julia Bolles-Wilson is currently Professor at the FH Münster.

Bolles + Wilson have won many national and international prizes, including: German Steel Prize 1976 (Julia Bolles and Hans Stadler), Shinken shiku competition Tokyo 1989 1st prize, Commendations in German Architecture Prize for Kita Frankfurt/Griesheim and Münster City Library, and a Gold Medal of the Japanese Architecture Institute for the Suzuki House 1994. Exhibitions include: Venice Biennale 1980, AA London 1980/84/89, Aedes Berlin 1989/97, Storefront New York 1990, Centre d'Architecture Bordeaux 1990, Westfälischer Kunstverein Münster 1993, GA Gallery Tokyo 1994, Phillipe Uzzan Paris 1995, Venice Biennale 1996.

Mitarbeiter 1994–97

Collaborators 1994–97

Nick Adomatis	Jateen Lad
Karl Amann	Jens Ludloff
Carole Asfour	Margherita Misitano
Katrin Becker	Cornelia Nottelmann
Dietmar Berner	Karola Päch
Elisabeth Böckenhoff-Diekmann	André Pannenbäcker
Anne Elshof	Michael Polte
Matthias Engemann	Wanda Richter
Laura Fogarasi	Marc Rips
Antje Giessmann	Martin Schlüter
Heike De Jonge-Ukena	Mark Schwesinger
Michael Kampkötter	Anke Stolberg
Axel Kempers	Jim Yohe
Andreas Kimmel	Jürgen Zils
Bettina Krakowski	Jörn Zschenker
Anja Kuhr	Eberhard Kleffner (Partner bis / until 1993)

Auswahlbibliographie
Selected Bibliography

1980	»The Presence of the Past«, Venice Biennial catalogue, Academy Editions, London.	03/94	Techniques & Architecture, no. 412, p. 106–107.
1984	Peter Wilson, »Bridgebuildings and the Shipshape«, AA Publications, Folio IV, London.	03/94	GA Houses, no. 41, p. 22–23.
		04/94	Architectura Viva, no. 35, p. 98–113.
06/86	»Vision der Moderne«, Deutsches Architektur-Museum, Ausstellungskatalog, München, p. 416–419.	10/94	»Bolles+Wilson«, El Croquis, no. 67.
		1994	Francisco Sanin, »Münster Library«, Phaidon, London.
11/88	Domus, no. 699, p. 58–64.	11/94	Lotus, no. 82, p. 68–75.
1990	GA Houses, no. 27, p. 22–35.	1995	Peter Wilson, »Eurolandschaft«, in: Die verstädterte Landschaft, Aries Verlag, München, p. 13–23.
1990	»Ouvertures«, catalogue, arc en rêve, Centre d'Architecture, Bordeaux, p. 3, 4, 8–11.		
1990	Peter Wilson, »Western Objects – Eastern Fields«, AA Publications, London.	01/95	Architecture, no. 84, p. 26–31, Sidney.
		05/95	Bauwelt, no. 17, p. 968–969.
03/91	»Architekturbüro Bolles+Wilson«, El Croquis, no. 47.	07/95	Domus, no. 773, p. 32–35.
		12/95	»Bolles+Wilson«, A+U, no. 303.
10/92	»Dimensions expanded explored«, exhibition catalogue, Rijksmuseum Kröller-Müller, Otterlo, p. 23.	1996	Peter Wilson, »Eurolandschaft«, in: The Idea of the City, AA Book, London, p. 100–107.
11/92	Telescope, no. 7, p. 56–70, Tokyo.	1996	Monument, no. 14, p. 66–81, Sidney.
01/93	Bauwelt, no. 5, p. 188–195.	1996	»La Biennale di Venezia«, Catalogue of the 6th International Architecture Exhibition, Electa, Milan, p. 174–175.
02/93	»Scuola Materna a Francoforte«, Domus, no. 746, p. 46–51.		
10/93	Architectural Review, no. 1160, p. 82–85.	08/96	Bauwelt, no. 31/32, p. 1776–1779.
10/93	»Bolles+Wilson Projekte 1988–1992«, Westfälischer Kunstverein, exhibition catalogue, Münster.	03/97	Domus, no. 791, p. 56–59.
		04/97	Architectural Review, no. 1202, p. 81–85.
11/93	»Stadtbücherei Münster«, Aedes-exhibition catalogue, Berlin.		
1994	Ole Baumann; Romer van Toorn, »The Invisible in Architecture«, Academy/Ernst & Sohn, Berlin, p. 236–243.		

Bildnachweis
Illustration Credits

Christian Richters, Münster:
Umschlagbild/cover picture, 7, 9, 19, 21, 22 oben/above, 23, 24, 25 oben/above, 26, 27, 28, 29, 30, 31, 33, 35, 36, 37, 38, 39, 40, 41, 43, 44, 45, 46, 47, 48, 49, 68, 69, 73, 75, 76, 77, 78, 79, 80, 81, 82, 85, 88, 89, 91 oben/above, 93, 94, 95, 96 rechts/right, 99, 100, 101, 105, 112 unten/below, 113 links/left.

Alle übrigen Illustrationen stammen aus dem Archiv von Bolles+Wilson, Münster.
All other illustrations are taken from the archive of Bolles+Wilson, Münster.

Die Herausgabe dieses Buches wurde unterstützt
von: / This publication was kindly supported by:

Brillux, Münster, Germany
Janinhoff GmbH & Co., Münster, Germany
WLV Westfälisch-Lippische Vermögensverwaltungs-
gesellschaft mbH, Münster, Germany
Zumtobel Staff, Lemgo, Germany

Übersetzungen ins Deutsche /
Translations into German: Julia Bolles-Wilson,
Wanda Richter

A CIP catalogue record for this book is available
from the Library of Congress, Washington D.C., USA

Deutsche Bibliothek Cataloging-in-Publication Data:

Architekturbüro Bolles-Wilson <Münster, Westfalen>:
Bolles + Wilson : neue Bauten und Projekte /
mit Photogr. von Christian Richters. [Übers. ins Dt.:
Julia Bolles-Wilson ; Wanda Richter]. - Basel ; Boston ;
Berlin : Birkhäuser, 1997
ISBN 3-7643-5610-3 (Basel ...)
ISBN 0-8176-5610-3 (Boston)

This work is subject to copyright. All rights are
reserved, whether the whole or part of the material
is concerned, specifically the rights of translation,
reprinting, re-use of illustrations, recitation, broad-
casting, reproduction on microfilms or in other ways,
and storage in data banks. For any kind of use,
permission of the copyright owner must be obtained.

© 1997 Birkhäuser – Verlag für Architektur,
P.O.Box 133, CH-4010 Basel, Switzerland
Printed on acid-free paper produced from
chlorine-free pulp. TCF ∞
Graphische Gestaltung und Umschlag /
Layout and cover design: Sabine an Huef, Kerken,
Germany
Printed in Italy
ISBN 3-7643-5610-3
ISBN 0-8176-5610-3

9 8 7 6 5 4 3 2 1